To Charles
my first sale!
Thanks,
Gregg Rickman

7-7-84
1st day of publication

PHILIP K. DICK:
IN HIS OWN WORDS
by Gregg Rickman

For My Mother

Published by **FRAGMENTS WEST/THE VALENTINE PRESS**
3908 East 4th Street,
Long Beach, California 90814
Copyright 1984 Gregg Rickman
All rights reserved. No portion of this book
may be used or reproduced in any form or by any
means without written permission of the author.
Introduction Copyright 1984 The Amber Corporation.
Letters Copyright 1984 Estate of Philip K. Dick
Used by permission
Printed in the United States of America.
ISBN No. 0-916063-01-1

IN HIS OWN WORDS : III

CONTENTS

INTRODUCTION, by Roger Zelazny
"Caught in the Movement of a Hand-Wound Universe"

A PREFACE AND THANKS

PART ONE: PHILIP K. DICK: AN INTRODUCTION

Chapter 1   A Biographical Note
1
Chapter 2   "Philip K. Dick and the Search for **Caritas**"
9   Introductory Note
11   One: Dick's Novels - A Pilgrim's Progress
16   Two: Dick's Heroes - Lost in the Maze
25   Three: Dick's Themes - The Search for **Caritas**
35   Four: Postscript (1984)
39   Comment, by Philip K. Dick
41   Notes

PART TWO: IN HIS OWN WORDS : WRITING SCIENCE FICTION

Chapter 3   Why Science Fiction? / The Benign Gods / Moral Choices
45
Chapter 4   **Caritas** / A Beetle in Third Grade / Cockroaches Are An
49   Exception / Seeing Things Five Different Ways

Chapter 5   Christian Beliefs / The Fallen World / C.S. Lewis /
53   Charles Williams / Olaf Stapleton / Benign Conspiraces /
                Tolkien.

Chapter 6   Earliest Writing / "I Love to Write" / Charybdis / Borges
57   Flaubert, Beethoven / Idioms

Chapter 7   "An Incredibly Conventional Writer" / The Early Stories /
63   The Form and the Craft / Markets of the Fifties /
                "Psionics" and John W. Campbell

Chapter 8   Donald Wollheim / Alternate Titles / Hard Science
67   Fiction

Chapter 9   The Sixties / Ellison and Wollheim / Origin of **Dr.**
75   **Bloodmoney / Dangerous Visions** / Hate Mail /
                Counterfeits

Chapter 10 Harlan Ellison / Reader Response / Publishers and
81   Agents / **Deus Irae** Censored

IV : PHILIP K. DICK

Chapter 11 Academic Critics / **Scanner** and Teilhard / Darko Suvin
87

Chapter 12 Multiple Viewpoints / Will Cook / Exploring All Possible
91 Viewpoints / James Joyce / Third Person Female

Chapter 13 Themes and Motifs: Hard Science / **Counter-Clock**
95 **World / Galactic Pot Healter** / Aliens / Desmesnes / Neanderthals / Policemen

Chapter 14 Fans and Fellow Writers / Disch and Spinrad / Michael
101 Moorcock and "The Skull" / Robert Silverberg / "Life is Predicated on Human Love" / (COMMENT BY ROBERT SILVERBERG)

Chapter 15 Ursula K. LeGuin / "Going Crazy in Santa Ana" /
107 "Unresolvable Metaphysical Problems" / "Hateful Women" / **The Lathe of Heaven** and **Ubik** / Phil's Sensitivity / (LETTER FROM URSULA K. LeGUIN) / Feminism and "The Pre-Persons"

PART THREE: THE NOVELS ONE BY ONE

Chapter 16 Self-Denial / "Kindly Death" / Ace Books
117

Chapter 17 The Early Novels: **Solar Lottery / The World Jones**
121 **Made / The Cosmic Puppets**

Chapter 18 The Early Novels: **The Man Who Japed / Eye in the Sky /**
127 Marxism / "Semi-Reality" / Race / An Old Black Man

Chapter 19 The Early Novels: **Time Out of Joint** / Gnosticism / The
137 Tao / **Vulcan's Hammer / Dr. Futurity** / Ray Bradbury

Chapter 20 The Literary Novels / **Confessions of a Crap Artist** /
143 Craftsmen, Intellectuals, Salesmen

Chapter 21 The Novels of the Early Sixties: **The Man in the High**
149 **Castle** / The Multi-Foci Format / A Sequel to **High Castle** / Nazis / Mussolini and **Now Wait for Last Year** / The Nature of Evil

Chapter 22 The Novels of the Early Sixties: "68 Pages a Day" /
156 **Martian Time Slip** / "I Had Found My Own Idiom" / **The Three Stigmata of Palmer Eldritch**

Chapter 23 The Novels of the Early Sixties : **The Simulacra / Clans**
162 **of the Alphane Moon / The Zap Gun** and **The Penultimate Truth** / "It Would Make a Great Film" / **Dr. Bloodmoney** / The Many Versions of **The Unteleported Man**

IN HIS OWN WORDS : V

Chapter 24　Hiatus / Writer's Block / **Now Wait for Last Year** and **The**
169　　　　**Crack in Space** / A Collaboration

Chapter 25　Ray Nelson / Writing **The Ganymede Takeover** /
173　　　　(INTERVIEW WITH RAY NELSON)

Chapter 26　The Novels of the Late Sixties: **Counter-Clock World** / "I
181　　　　Was Very Happy" / **Do Androids Dream of Electric**
　　　　　　Sheep? and **Ubik** / "Ossification": **A Maze of Death** and
　　　　　　Our Friends from Frolix 8 / The **Ubik** Screenplay /
　　　　　　Galactic Pot Healer / **We Can Build You**

Chapter 27　The Early Seventies: Hiatus / **Flow My Tears, the**
188　　　　**Policeman Said** / "Writing Autobiographically" / **Deus**
　　　　　　Irae and Roger Zelazny

Chapter 28　The Late Seventies: **A Scanner Darkly** / The Drug
193　　　　Culture: "I Want to Record Them" / Donna / **VALIS**

Chapter 29　**The Divine Invasion** / "A Pleasure to Write" / A Sequel to
199　　　　**VALIS** / A Study of Judaism / Muzak and Linda Ronstadt

PART FOUR: THE LAST YEAR

Chapter 30　The Scott Meredith Agency / Discursive Writing / Russ
207　　　　Galen and Bishop Archer

Chapter 31　Writing **Timothy Archer**: The First Three Pages / A
211　　　　Woman as Protagonist / John Lennon's Death / Religious
　　　　　　Mania / "My Poor Agent" / Harvey the Cat / Angel Archer
　　　　　　/ A Good Book

Chapter 32　The Making of **Blade Runner** / Ridley Scott / "I Don't
222　　　　Want To Do The Goddamned Novelization" / Rewriting a
　　　　　　"Joke Screenplay" / "They Did Sight Stimulation on My
　　　　　　Brain" / Good Grass / Science Fiction as Futurism / "I
　　　　　　Was Ecstatic" / My Little Boy / A Near Great Film

Chapter 33　**The Owl in Daylight**
237
Chapter 34　"We Die Too Soon"
241

VI : PHILIP K. DICK

APPENDICES

A 244	The Novels of Philip K. Dick Short Story Collections
B 246	Bibliography Interviews with Philip K. Dick Books on Philip K. Dick Miscellaneous References
C 249	Two Letters from Philip K. Dick June 26, 1981 June 29, 1981

* * * * *

INTRODUCTION
by Roger Zelazny
Caught in the Movement of a Hand-Wound Universe

Reading this collection of interviews with Philip K. Dick has brought back to mind conversations we had over the years. It has also reminded me of his life. Not so much the substance as the style. Phil was a humorist - a bizarre one, to be sure - alternately employing the grotesque, the ironic, the slapstick. He was attracted by the possibilities of

VIII : PHILIP K. DICK

situations of this ilk in his fiction, and he tended to view his life and life in general along these lines, at least in conversation and correspondence. It also seems that he somehow personally attracted happenings of this sort.

I've listened to him take ten minutes to construct a byzantine chain of reasoning to interpret some political or philosophical point. Someone would then try poking a few holes in it, and he always had an answer in keeping with the tenor of the piece. Finally, when a head would nod and someone would say, "Maybe you have a point there," he would pause, catch his breath and say, "But no...Maybe **you** were right..." and then set off discrediting his construct to substitute something completely different and just as peculiar. It seemed that whenever he began approaching certainty he would feel uncomfortable, draw back and find an ambiguity to pursue in its stead. It was an intellectual dance, an eternal approaching with never an arrival. It was very amusing, and he knew it. It was also extremely difficult to know just how serious or playful it might be at any given time. It made me think about his stories and his characters: pathos mixed with the ludicrous, the sudden abandonment of ideas to flirt with alternatives, near-surrealistic scenes that sometimes seemed objectifications of neuroses, characters generally more acted upon than acting, sex without a great deal of pleasure...He once told me in a letter, "Kafka is a favorite of mine, and I have long wished I could utilize some of his methods in my own s.f. -- but so far I've failed." I wasn't at all certian he'd missed by much. He also liked Becket, and our last few telephone conversations touched upon the possibility of our collaborating on a book based on an idea he liked in a story by Borges. How strong might have been the influence of any or all of these writers upon him is impossible to say. It's one of those chicken-or-egg things. Did he like them because he was learning from them? Or was he drawn to them because he was already informed with something much like their approaches to story-telling and felt a certain kinship? I suspect the latter, and I am always leary of hunts for literary influences, anyway. Phil had his own existential dance, with pratfalls. I like to think he was also his own choreographer.

There was some demonstration of this dance in his own life, one instance of which I was present to witness, occurring in Metz, France in the autumn of 1977, at the Second International Science Fiction Festival. The sponsors of the event had brought over three U.S. sf writers -- Philip K. Dick, Harlan Ellison and myself. Phil was to give the major guest address, several days into the event. Of necessity, he wrote it out beforehand. It had to be translated into French, so that he could read a paragraph in English to be followed immediately by the translator's reading the same passage in French. The day arrived. I could not be present at the talk because I had been scheduled to begin an autograph party at a local bookstore, to be joined later by Phil, when we would both sign copies of the French edition of **Deus Irae.**

My first inkling that something peculiar had occurred came when a couple of French fans associated with the Festival came into the store arguing with each other and looking puzzled. They approached me at the table where I was signing books.

"M'sieu Zelazny," one of them said, "you have worked with M'sieu Dick and you know his mind. Does he really wish to found his own religion with himself as Pope?"

"He'd never mentioned it to me," I said.

He turned triumphantly and said something to the other in rapid-fire French which I couldn't follow.

Then the other addressed me: "But I rode with him in the taxi back to the hotel and he gave me the power to remit sins -- and to kill fleas."

"It was a joke," I said. "You can't always tell when he's joking. But it was a joke."

"I am not so sure," he replied.

Then the first one asked me, "Do you believe - as M'sieu Dick does - that God and the Devil are playing a game of chess for the fate of the universe, and that every time one of Them makes a move reality is altered?"

I cleared my throat to begin a reply, but he continued, "...And that every time Phil Dick writes a book reality is switched back to its normal track for a time. **Deus Irae** has done it most recently, he said. Eh?"

"Phil had never mentioned that one to me either," I said. "But, again, you must realize that his sense of humor may not always come through so well in translation."

He shook his head.

"I am not so sure," he said.

More people who had been present at the talk began drifting in. They all had similar odd questions for me on the working of Phil's mind and the structure of his personal philosophy. I kept parrying them. Finally, Phil showed up, looking harassed, sat down beside me and began signing books.

"Phil, just what the hell did you talk about today?" I asked him.

"I don't know," he replied.

"Really," I said. "I've been getting a lot of weird questions about it."

"I really don't know," he said.

"What do you mean?" I asked. "You wrote the damned speech."

"But it's not the one I gave," he answered. Then, "Well, it was. But it wasn't the one they heard."

"Oh?" I said. "What happened?"

"I had to cut it," he told me. "They were running late and

they asked me to shorten it by twenty minutes."

"So?"

"I went through it and crossed out sections. My translator did the same, but his copy was set up differently and he didn't cross out the same sections. I don't know which ones he crossed out, though, and which ones were retained. I don't read French."

"Nobody from the audience is certain what you said."

He nodded.

"Neither am I."

I suddenly felt as if I were in the middle of a Phil Dick story. He had been brought around the world to give a talk, it had been given and now everyone had a different view as to what had been said.

And the author was powerless to interpret...

A lady came up to the table.

"Let me introduce myself," she said in English. "I am Francoise Cartano. I did the French translation of **Deus Irae**, and I wanted to apologize to you."

"What for?" we asked.

"I was rushed," she said, "and I didn't realize it until it was too late - when the book was already printed - that in places I gave Tibor McMasters a 4-wheeled cart, and in other places it has only two wheels. I'm very sorry."

"That's all right," Phil said. "It's kind of a nice touch. Says something about reality."

We signed a lot of books that afternoon. Phil is very popular in France. I wondered a lot about life imitating art. Not just anybody's art. Phil Dick's art. Wouldn't it be appropriate if his presence really rubbed the fabric of Maya so thin that the Chaos leaked through? Whatever, it was an instructive privilege to inhabit a Philip K. Dick story for those few brief hours and to know that it was not a paranoid vision, by his definition:

XII : PHILIP K. DICK

> Sudden surprises, by the way - and this thought may be in itself a sudden surprise to you - are a sort of antidote to the paranoid...or, to be accurate about it, to live in such a way as to encounter sudden surprises quite often or even now and then is an indication that you are not paranoid, because to the paranoid, nothing is a surprise; everything seems exactly as he has expected, and sometimes even more so. It all fits into his system. For us, though, there can be no system; maybe **all** systems - that is any theoretical, verbal symbolic, semantic, etc. formulation that attempts to act as an all-encompassing, all-explaining hypothesis of what the universe is about - are manifestations of paranoia. We should be content with the mysterious, the meaningless, the contradictory, the hostile, and most of all the unexplainably warm and giving - total so-called inanimate environment, in other words very much like a person, like the behavior of one intricate, subtle, half-veiled, deep, perplexing, and much-to-be-loved human being to another. To be feared a little, too, sometimes. And perpetually misunderstood. About which we can neither know nor be sure; and we must only trust and make guesses toward. Not being what you thought, not doing right by you, not being just, but then sustaining you as by momentary caprice, but then abandoning you, or at least seeming to. What it is actually up to we may never know.

He'd said that in his Vancover guest of honor speech in 1972. I'd often wondered about it, as it seemed to leave very little in which to believe. But then, he admits this. In a letter describing a positive aspect of his work (to **SF Commentary** #17, 1970), he said:

> I know only one thing about my novels. In them, again and again, this minor man asserts himself in all his hasty, sweaty strength. In the ruins of Earth's cities he is busily constructing a little factory that turns out cigars or maps or imitation artifacts that say, "Welcome to Miami, the pleasure center of the world." In **A.Lincoln,Simulacrum** he operates a little business that produces corny electronic organs -- and, later on, human-like robots which ultimately become more of an irritation than a threat. Everything is on a small scale. Collapse is enormous; the positive little figure outlined against the universal rubble is,

like Tagomi, Runciter, Molinari, gnat-sized in scope, finite in what he can do...and yet in some sense great. I really do not know why. I simply believe in him and I love him. He will prevail. There is nothing else. At least nothing else that matters. That we should be concerned about. Because if he is there, like a tiny father-figure, everything is all right.

Some reviewers have found "bitterness" in my writing. I am surprised, because my mood is one of trust. Perhaps they are bothered by the fact that what I trust is so very small. They want something vaster. I have news for them: there is nothing vaster. Nothing **more,** I should say. But really, how much do we have to have? Isn't Mr. Tagomi enough? Isn't what he does enough? I know it counts. I am satisfied.

He was a strange and wonderful man. I liked his cockeyed visions, his near-nihilistic dances of ideas, that final touch of idealism. He was scary, amusing and sometimes profound. There was a kind of catharsis in his best works, such as **Ubik, Do Androids Dream of Electric Sheep?** and **Dr. Bloodmoney.** I miss him. I doubt Time will ever deliver another writer quite like him. But, as he once said in a poetry fragment:

Why did clocks bring man into the world?
Only to amuse?
(Knowing clocks, would this be strange?)

* * * * *

Introduction ©1984 The Amber Corporation.

XIV: PHILIP K. DICK

A PREFACE AND THANKS
by Gregg Rickman

"In the final analysis, life is predicated on human love, mutual human love."
-- Philip K. Dick (1928-1982)

There are people who profoundly affect our lives who we never meet -- artists, usually, whose work gets into our bloodstream, who we absorb and who become a part of ourselves. When we first encounter their work, be it in music heard over the radio or in a book casually picked up in some supermart book stall, we feel an instant cathexis with them, a union, and for a while, for a few months at least, we drunkenly gulp every record they made or painting they painted, until the fever has run its course.

And then you can truly appreciate the artist. Then you can stand back and see how their perceptions, their vision of life has entered into you and subtly changed the very rhythms of your heart. There must first have been some unknown and unspoken link between you before luck or search helped you make the connection -- you have to have in some way prepared yourself for the communion, to have held yourself open for it. It can't be forced (or, this is why high school kids hate Hamlet. All teachers can do is prepare their students, to teach them to be ready).

Besides the artists we never meet there are, even more importantly, the artists of life we have as friends. A teacher, a brother, a parent, a pal, a lover, a student, a son or a daughter can open you up to shadings of life you could never have known. The operative word is "friend." If each of us carries within ourselves a universe all to our own, imagine the universes carried within the bus of strangers you ride with each morning? A friend is someone with whom you co-mingle universes. A friend is someone who cares enough about you -- no strike that, a friend is someone who is interested enough in you to learn to care about you. A friendship is more than curiosity, less than love at first sight. Love itself is friendship by another name.

In my life I have been profoundly affected by a number of artists, profoundly affected more by a number of friends. There is but one man who was both great artist and friend to me, and he is the late Philip K. Dick. A science fiction writer, I got to know him first in his weird, great, off-the-wall and masterly science fiction novels, mostly paperback

XVI : PHILIP K. DICK

originals, with titles like **Galactic Pot-Healer** and **Counter-Clock World, Eye in the Sky** and **Do Androids Dream of Electric Sheep?**

I had seen and read parts of Phil's books before. I read some of **Ubik** when I was 14, standing around waiting for my mother in the upstairs Book Department of the South Bay May Company, circa 1970. I read all of **Man in the High Castle** in my first year of college, circa 1974. I was impressed, but went on to other things.

The enthusiasms of my childhood were Oz books and dinosaurs, then the Peanuts books and American history, the constellations as drawn by H.A. Rey and then in 1968 the complete works of George Orwell. 1970 was the year I discovered Buster Keaton, and with him the cinema. In '72 and '73 Bach was joined by Fats Waller and Jelly Roll Morton. They all changed the way I saw and thought. 1980 found me adrift in San Francisco, a would-be great artist stumbling around insular colonies of artists and actors and shoveling tofu to the upwardly mobile at the Real Foods Health Food Store, Polk Street branch. One night, downwardly mobile myself, I was pushing my way uphill to my Bush Street apartment when I came across a book store I had never seen before, a tiny Used Paperbacks for Sale store front called Twice Read Tales, 682 Post Street. There I browsed and found three novels by Philip K. Dick, **Solar Lottery, The Penultimate Truth,** and **Flow My Tears, the Policeman Said** -- one novel each as it happened from each decade of Phil's writing career.

I bought them and I read them, remembering back to **Ubik** and **High Castle** so long ago. I read them over breakfast granola, a tasty flakey kind I can't find anymore and which came in great plastic sacks. I read them over the boiled potatoes I mashed for supper. I read them at night, real late, aggressive San Francisco roaches and black beetles patrolling the edge of my lamp light. I read them on the BART train scooting over to Berkeley, where there were more used book stores with more Phil Dick books.

I read them all. All 29 (as of 1980. He wrote three more before he died). Plus five collections of short stories. What I loved about his work - still do - was not the worlds of collapsing realities he so skillfully created and which most prize him for. I loved him for the love he showed his characters, even in extremis, even when they didn't deserve it.

I wrote a long essay and said so. A friend gave me Phil's address. He lived, of all places, in Santa Ana. I sent a copy of my essay to Phil and when I was down visiting in Long Beach for a month (April 1981) he called me up and said how much he liked it.

And so I met Phil Dick.

* * * * *

Over the next year, the last of his life, I met with and interviewed Phil Dick five times. We also talked on the phone and corresponded. I gathered 16 hours of tape recorded interviews, Phil on all subjects: his life, science fiction, politics, his visions. I went through his correspondence on file at the Fullerton State archives, compiling many pages of notes.

I met him in April 1981. He gave an overview of his career, explained why he liked to write science fiction.

I met him again in September, and twice in October. He went over each of his novels one-by-one, talked about his visions (as reported in his 1981 novel **VALIS** and elsewhere), and talked about his life. He was haunted all his life by a twin sister who died in infancy -- they are buried together now.

Each time I saw him he seemed more frail, less robust, less happy. On my last October visit he showed me how to read the **I Ching** and then sent me home. He was ill in

XVIII : PHILIP K. DICK

November, December, January. I saw him again in February 1982, a marathon session that chiefly concerned itself with Phil's anger at Reagan, the Russians, and the chemical destruction of Earth - and his professed belief in the imminent return of Christ.

Phil Dick was not, as some have claimed, "spiraling into madness" in the last years of his life. To the end he maintained perspective on his most outrageous claims, wit among the anger, alternate explanations for every vision. He was however, burning himself up in his love for the world and the life within it. I saw him then and I see him now as a martyr of empathy.

I saw the scars on Phil's arm one day in November 1981, shortly after Anwar Sadat had been assassinated. When he heard the news, Phil said, he crushed his soda pop can and scraped his skin until he just drew blood. He was not crazy, Phil said, for he then immediately washed his arm and applied disinfectant. But he felt the need to share the pain of Sadat's death - a martyr to peace. He had the Old Testament need for a blood sacrifice - only, as in the New Testament, he sacrificed himself.

And again -- he could be hilarious. When I typed up these transcripts of Phil's interviews I was coninually typing in (laughter) after one or another of Phil's deadpan sorties into the absurd. Phil was also profoundly intelligent. Essentially self-educated, he had acquired profound knowledge of history, philosophy, and religion. And Phil was extremely kind. Each of my visits were devoted in part to his questions about how I was doing. He bought me sandwiches, he brewed me coffee, he was always extremely complimentary about my writing.

* * * * *

Phil's death left me numb. He was feeling badly the last evening I talked to him. I offered to stay the night with him but he sent me home; I called him when I got there and he said he was feeling better. The next morning a neighbor saw him go out to get the paper. That same day he had a stroke. Taken to the hospital, he was begining to rally when he had another, more massive stroke, and then another. He died ten days after I last saw him, on March 2, 1982. I - who had been calling him and getting no answer for several days - heard about his death that night.

For the next year or so - I had determined to write a biography of Phil, and had in fact told him so, to his approval - I traveled on my vacations and breaks from work and interviewed a number of those who knew him. His father, who was 82. Three of his five ex-wives. His half-sister. His collaborator, Ray Nelson, on one novel (**The Ganymede Takeover**). And others. Every last soul thought highly of Phil, even when there had been rifts and misunderstandings between them.

But it seemed there were so many versions of Phil's truth I was beginning to despair of ever settling on one, The Truth. And then it came to me -- let Phil speak for himself. And so I am.

* * * * *

This book is the first of three projected volumes of Philip K. Dick speaking in his own words. This volume is Phil speaking on his career as a science fiction writer, on each of his books and also, inescapably, on the biographical and philosophical elements lying behind each novel. Volume Two, **Philip K. Dick: The Last Testament** will incorporate Phil's last tape, made the day in February 1982 before he had his stroke, and will cover all of his extraordinary visions and his many statements and thoughts on religion and philosophy -- the things that mattered most to him in life, which his novels merely animated. The two books are closely interwoven but have their distinct and separate uses. Both may be read by the general reader, for I have taken pains to explain each reference. The day may come when Phil's reputation as a philosopher exceeds his (large and growing) reputation as a science fiction writer. He would be amused.

Volume Three, projected for publication at some point in 1985 (probably the summer), will attempt to untangle the threads of Phil's extraordinary life. It will include, in addition to Phil's memoirs of his life as told to me, the interviews I have made with various of Phil's relatives and friends and further interviews I hope to make with more who knew him. If anyone reading this book knew Phil and would like to talk with me, please contact me via my publisher at:

FRAGMENTS WEST
3908 East 4th Street
Long Beach, California 90814

I would appreciate it.

* * * * *

In transcribing Phil's talks with me for publication, I have made every effort to not only accurately reproduce what Phil said, but to capture the style of his spoken speech, which was extraordinarily rich and dense with allusion. He was an incredible conversationalist and great interview; my contributions as editor have been merely to elide some repetitions and, by the ordering of chapters, and occasional juxtapositions of statements made on different dates, place chronological and topical fences around his talk for the benefit of readers. Any deletion of material of more than a line or two - frequently philosophical digressions that I am shunting off into Volume Two - is marked by an ellipsis (...), which occurs for no other reason in the main body of text. (Five stars * * * * * mark a break in the recording or a change in topic, or a return to the same topic after a lively digression).

Within the body of the interviews (Parts Two-Four), anything found in parentheses is an editorial comment or clarification by me. Thus if anyone were to listen to the original tapes side by side with reading the text, they would find Phil's language reproduced almost word for word, with my editorial comments and phrasing of my questions comprising almost all of the different materials. (While leaving Phil's language intact I have often reworded my questions, to give the reader more information, or simply to make myself sound coherent). I have also added occasional parenthetical comments such as (laughter) or (angry) to indicate the tone of Phil's conversation, a tone that could shift very quickly indeed.

Finally, four people who knew Phil - Robert Silverberg, Ursula LeGuin, Ray Nelson, and in his marvelous introduction Roger Zelazny - have allowed me to fold their comments on Phil into this volume. I thank them all very much.

* * * * *

Beyond the people who are actually quoted within a book the people who help an author create the book deserve thanks and credit. I would like to thank:

My mother and my father, for their unfailing kindness, love, and generosity;

Paul Williams, executor of Phil Dick's estate, for his generous encouragement and aid in clearing rights to material;

Tim Powers, another friend of Phil's, who along with Paul helped me out with my fact checking;

Bill Blackbeard, proprietor of the San Francisco Academy of Comic Art, for giving me Phil's address back in 1981 and in a sense starting this whole project;

Anne, Nancy, and Tessa Dick, Mr. and Mrs. Edgar Dick, and the other friends and relatives of Phil I've interviewed;

Phil Yeh, my publisher, and his associates at Cobblestone Gallery, for their faith in this project and their willingness to put up their time and their money to see it become real;

Rex Strother, my typesetter, for not making any mistakes in putting my perfect manuscript into print (I am writing this before Rex has actually set any copy so we shall see how inspired he is by this dedication);

William Mitchell, who picked it all up and laid it all down;

Judy, Hilde, Arlene, Linda, Mary, and Rosey of the Alamitos Branch Library, for putting up with me at work while I was actually thinking about this work;

All of my other friends inside the library and out, just for being my friends;

All of the friends of Phil Dick I have talked to, and those I have never met -- this book belongs to you, too;

And most of all to the late Phil Dick, my friend. What can I say? I loved the guy.

> Gregg Rickman
> Long Beach, California
> April 1984

PART ONE:
Philip K. Dick:
An Introduction

CHAPTER 1
A Biographical Note

Philip Kindred Dick was born on December 16, 1928, in Chicago, Illinois. His father, Joseph Edgar Dick (b. 1899), fought World War I in France and eventually became Secretary of the California Cattlemen's Association. His mother, born Dorothy Kindred, held responsible posts in the forestry service.

Philip Dick was born with a twin sister, Jane, who died

January 26, 1929. Her brief life, and death, had a profound effect on her brother's life. (This question is gone into in the second book of this series).

The family moved to California in 1929. Phil's parents separated when he was 4½. (Divorced 1935). Phil and his mother relocated to Washington, D.C., where he attended - most unhappily - a Virginia military academy and other schools through fourth grade. They then moved again, eventually settling in Berkeley, California.

Graduating from high school there, and seeing publication for the first time in the **Berkeley Gazette** "Young Author's Club" (1944), he developed a passion for classical music. He worked briefly for KSMO Radio, San Mateo, and, very formatively, for a record store in Berkeley whose owner was a father figure to him and the apparent model for the recurring figure, in Dick's novels, of the heroic small businessman (Leo Bulero, Jim Fergesson).

In 1948 Phil Dick briefly attended UC Berkeley, dropping out rather than take mandatory ROTC. (His disgust with the snobbish attitude of the intelligencia on campus also played a part in this decision. See Chapter 20).

Phil was briefly married, in 1949-50, to Jeannette Marlin, and in 1951 he married again, to Kleo Apostolides. His 1980 introduction to **The Golden Man** paints a vivid portrait of his life in poverty in the 1950's, struggling to make ends meet as a writer. At the end of 1951 he sold his first story, "Beyond Lies the Wub," to **Planet Stories,** and very shortly thereafter quit his job as record clerk to write full time.

Writing rapidly, and increasingly skillfully, he soon became established as a short story author in the science fiction field. He acquired Scott Meredith as his literary agent, and stayed with the agency for the rest of his life. From 1951 through 1960, he struggled to sell one of the many non-science fiction, literary novels he wrote, but failed to place any of them. This disappointment lingered for many years, being soothed with the 1975 publication of **Confessions of a Crap Artist** (1959) and the acceptance, shortly before his death, of a new literary novel, **The Transmigration of Timothy Archer** (1982).

It was in science fiction, though, that Phil Dick made his literary mark. After hitting peaks of 30 and 28 stories respectively published in 1953 and 1954, he moved into novel writing with the very successful **Solar Lottery** (1955), first of many paperback originals published by Ace Books and its canny science fiction editor, Donald Wollheim. He produced one or two novels a year through the rest of the decade, including his first hardcover novel, **Time Out of Joint** (1959).

In 1957 he divorced Kleo and in 1958 married Anne Williams Rubenstein, moving to live with her in isolated West Marin County, in Point Reyes Station. (Their elaborate homestead is described quite accurately in **Confessions of a Crap Artist**). One child, Laura, was born in 1960; Phil also doted on his step-fatherhood of Anne's daughters from her first marriage, Hatte, Jayne, and Tandy.

Unhappy with his inability to break out of the science fiction field - which was undergoing, in any event, a tremendous slump - Phil, briefly, gave up writing in 1960-61, helping his wife set up her jewelry business (which is still thriving). Even more unhappy not writing, he threw himself into producing the novel many still consider his greatest, **The Man in the High Castle** (1962).

This novel winning him the very prestigious Hugo Award for Best Novel of its year, Phil launched himself into his most prolific period yet, publishing no less than four novels in 1964 alone. His marriage to Anne broke up, however, that same year (the divorce was officially 1966). He moved to Oakland and underwent his first serious spell of writer's block -- although this may have been more in the way of exhaustion, and recharging of creative batteries.

Meeting, and in 1967 marrying, his fourth wife Nancy Hackett (break-up 1970, divorce 1972, one child, Isolde, born 1967) allowed the author a short-lived breathing spell in which he produced some of his best, and least recognized work: **Counter-Clock World** (1967), **Galactic Pot Healer** (1969), the widely acclaimed **Ubik** (1969), and **Do Androids Dream of Electric Sheep?** (1968). This last novel was to serve as the basis for the Hollywood feature film, **Blade Runner** (1982), the making of which preoccupied Phil at times in the last months of his life.

Over the years Phil Dick moved through many widely disparate circles of friends: the antithetical groups of Communists, record store employees, and poets of his Berkeley days; the science fiction community described by his colleague Ray Nelson in Chapter 25 and the "counter culture" drug users he took up with after he and Nancy moved to San Rafael in 1968. (And particularly after Nancy left in 1970).

More nonsense has been written on Philip Dick's usage of drugs than on any other topic relating to him (though a tally of misrepresentations that he was "crazy" in his last years may top the old record any day now). The facts appear to be that he was a heavy user of amphetamines for twenty years, from the early fifties through about 1973. He used them, he said, to keep up his writing speed, which was indeed prodigious, and always claimed that his supply was legal (he was apparently over-prescribed by one or more psychiatrists). Although he has a heavy reputation as an "acid head" novelist, he took LSD only two or three times, and not 'til about 1967 (his famous "LSD novel" **The Three Stigmata of Palmer Eldritch** was in fact written and published some years before this).

The shifting, collapsing realities Philip K. Dick's novels are famous for presenting stem more from the author's own amazing imagination - and life - than from any drugs he ingested. (In fact, he once claimed in an interview that medical examination had proved his liver had "detoxified" the amphetamines he took before they reached his brain! It is true that he did suffer serious liver and pancreatic damage from his habit).

It was more a romantic identification with the "anti-Establishment" aura of the dope culture youth Phil Dick ran with in 1970-72, than attachment to drugs, that led Phil to make his home "open house" to runaways and drifters galore in those years. Phil always claimed that he learned a great deal from these youth, and was heartened and astounded by their heroism; others say he was horribly used and ripped-off by this element; and probably both sides are right. Phil was never at ease with authority - witness his career-long obsession with policemen (Chapter 13) - and in about 1968 he cemented his anti-Establishment status by participating in an anti-war act he professed to be afraid to tell me what it was as late as 1981. (I believe it was merely income tax evasion; in any event he did settle a big bill with the IRS in the seventies).

In November 1971, Phil's house was blown open, entered, and ransacked, by an unknown force, variously speculated to be government agents, a secret right-wing organization, a secret **left**-wing organization, drug-mad youth, and Phil himself. (Paul Williams' article in **Rolling Stone** - see Appendix B for Bibliography - has the most complete set of speculations on record on this mystery, never solved). The fact that the house-breakers left valuables and took Phil's cancelled checks going back twenty years would tend to indicate that the hit was indeed politically motivated.

In February 1972, Phil Dick fled to Vancouver, Canada, where as guest of honor at a science fiction convention there (March 1972) he delivered the important address, "The Android and the Human," a summary, he said, of a lifetime of his thought. There was a suicide attempt, followed by a month in a very strict drug rehabilitation center in Vancouver called X-Kalay.

He took the opportunity of an offer from Cal State University, Fullerton, to store his papers and manuscripts in the library there, to leave Canada and what he felt was a too-strict regimen. From the spring of 1972 and for the rest of his life he was a resident of the great flat suburbs of Orange County, California, with a new circle of friends (prominently including authors Tim Powers and K.W. Jeter) and a new series of intense relationships.

In 1973 he married Tessa Busby, not yet 20, and a son, Christopher, was born within a year. He began writing again, completing his renunciation of the drug scene with the extremely intense and brilliantly pure **A Scanner Darkly** (1977). This marriage, however, broke up as well (in 1976) and after a second botched suicide attempt (described in Chapter 4 of his novel **VALIS**), he settled with some serenity into a condo apartment a few blocks from Santa Ana Civic Center, his last home.

The dominant event of the last years of his life, overshadowing all else, was however the "VALIS events" of February-March 1974. Put as concisely as possible, he felt that he had seen God, or a manifestation of God - perhaps a God greater than the "creator deity" who had done such a bad job with this planet. Feeling that he had been allowed to see everything but that he'd been denied understanding of it, he filled over the next years a handwritten journal of two million words (the "Exegesis"), analyzing his visions in exhaustive detail, and more crucially in terms of his art spun a wise and sane book out of this madness, **VALIS** (1981).

Thus the rumors of Phil's "insanity," spread by any

number of eager voices through the science fiction community and beyond. The groundwork of this picture of Phil Dick as mad visionary was already being laid, of course, by such widely reported earlier visions of his as his seeing a "Palmer Eldritch face in the sky" (1963), the acidhead image of the late '60s, and his own amazing work. For toppers, there was a late vision of a suffering Christ-like "Tagore" in Sri Lanka (reported to me and others in 1981), and his involvement in the last months of his life with an organization claiming to publicize the imminent return of "Maitreya the Christ."

This book is being written to help establish, or solidify, Philip K. Dick's reputation as a great writer, by having him relate in his own words his struggles and triumphs as an author. I am devoting the second book of this series, **Philip K. Dick: The Last Testament,** to the extraordinary record of his visions, and intend to prove in there, that Phil Dick was far from insane - it are we who are likely insane for laughing him off. The visions of the last decade of his life were not those of a madman spiraling into insanity, but of a supremely seeing human being burning himself up, physically and spiritually, with his empathy for the whole human race. Let who will read these books and laugh then.

To conclude the data of Phil's life - he continued, in his Santa Ana "high castle," writing and thinking up until Thursday, February 18, 1982. He had much to look forward to - the publication of his Timothy Archer novel (based on his close friendship with the late Bishop Jim Pike and his circle in the late sixties), the release of **Blade Runner,** the enjoyment of new fame and prosperity as a science fiction writer. The years of starvation and neglect had given way to recognition.

On that day he had a stroke, followed by a more severe stroke and a heart attack. He died on March 2nd.

8 : PHILIP K. DICK

CHAPTER 2
Philip K. Dick and The Search for Caritas

INTRODUCTORY NOTE
   This is the essay which first served to introduce me to Philip K. Dick. I am publishing it here because he liked it, and because it forms the backdrop for most of this book. It serves as well, I think, as a pretty fair survey of Phil Dick's work as a writer.

The piece as it stands reads essentially as Phil read it in the spring of 1981. I have corrected errors, updated it with an afterword covering the two books he published after **VALIS,** and used the footnotes to open the piece out to other references, in this book and elsewhere.

The article may be read as a supplement to the conversations that make up most of this book, or as background for them. In itself, it is for me a sweet souvenir of the year I knew Phil Dick. There is no "past tense" to my statement "Philip K. Dick is a great writer."

-- G.R., 1984

* * * * *

"Basically, I am not serene."
-- Philip K. Dick [1]

Philip K. Dick is a great writer, one of the greatest we have. His greatness is not a function of beautiful prose, stylistic innovation, his status in the field of science fiction, his influence on others, or even his incredible imagination. He has deservedly won recognition in some degree for all of these things. But where his real greatness lies is in the love and care he has for his most tortured characters, and his understanding of their pain. His empathy. Or, as he so frequently calls it in his books, **caritas.**

This view of Dick has not been central to the critical work on him thus far, but it is one that imposes itself after a careful reading of his work, with special attention paid to what Dick himself has to say about it. Dick's recent work has become ever more personal, the philosophizing ever more explicit, 'til where **VALIS** (1981) includes both scholarly footnotes, and Dick himself as a character.

For all that, **VALIS** is fully in line with the overriding concerns of Dick's earlier books, stories, essays, and interviews. It also contains links to the great body of Dickian themes, variants, and motifs, the most important of which we will detail here.

In the first part of this essay, however, we will trace the linear development of Dick's career, one beginning some thirty years ago with the publication of his first story ("Beyond Lies the Wub," 1952). Wub-fur coats and wub-bound books have recurred in Dick's writing ever since that first story about a fat, furry creature who'd rather philosophize than die. Not all of Dick's recurring themes are tragic.

ONE: Dick's Novels - A Pilgrim's Progress

Critical work on Dick to date has emphasized the prolific imagination that led him to publish six books in 1964 alone, and a total of nineteen (plus twenty-two stories) in 1962-70. "He can strike more sparks from an idea he's used in six books already than most of us can from a notion we've never encountered before," wrote John Brunner in one of the first appraisals of his work.[2] Stanislaw Lem praised Dick with faint damns for "resurrecting" what he considered the science fictional "trash" of androids, precogs, psi-powers (and he might have added time travel, alternate universes, space ships, alien invasions, and the World-after-the-Bomb, other genre staples Dick has made his own). To Lem, this "trash" recovers in Dick's hands its "long-extinct, metaphysical-exotic value,"[3] which is another way of saying that Dick takes the religious, moral, and philosophical consequences of quasi-scientific miracles seriously.

Dick's reputation in the science fiction community still rests largely on his pre-1965 work, notably the novels **Eye in the Sky** (1957), **Time Out of Joint** (1959 , the Hugo-award winner **The Man in the High Castle** (1962), **Martian Time-Slip** and **Dr. Bloodmoney** (1965). Of the later novels only **Ubik** (1969) is considered major Dick by most of his commentators.[4]

It is my contention, however, that Dick's richest period came after those dazzling early works (and others as good - **The Cosmic Puppets, The Game Players of Titan, Clans of the Alphane Moon).** Dick's finest, most humane and beautiful flowering comes in the neglected novels **Now Wait for Last Year, Counter-Clock World, Galactic Pot Healer,** the "policeman trilogy" of **Do Androids Dream of Electric Sheep?, Flow My Tears, the Policeman Said,** and **A Scanner Darkly,** and a half-dozen others nearly as good, all published in the years 1966 to 1977. More recently **VALIS** (1981) is that flowering plucked, ground under, and then reborn.

Schematically, I will break Dick's progress as a novelist

towards the startling self-portrait, in **VALIS,** of "Horse-lover Fat," whose empathy is killing him, into four distinct periods. Anomalies, of course, break up such easy categorization - **Our Friends from Frolix 8** (1970), for example, would seem to link up with **The Game Players of Titan** and **Clans of the Alphane Moon,** from 1963-64, as part of an "alien invasion" trilogy. But of course **Titan** also links with **Solar Lottery** (1955) - "game players" - and with **The Penultimate Truth** (1964) - huge tracts of land being fought for on a depopulated planet. **Clans of the Alphane Moon** looks back to the story "Shell Game" (1954) and ahead to **A Maze of Death** (1970) in its concerns with the murderous workings of a literally insane, isolated society. Where it really counts **Frolix** does belong in its period, because it does link up with the surrounding volumes (the comic **Galactic Pot-Healer** and the tragic **A Maze of Death**) in the overriding concern of Dick at the time for a God-figure coming to save us, to join with us in "poly-encephalic fusion," to literally swallow us.

I have suggested above the density of the cross-referencing in Dick's work. But it does progress in distinct phases, thus:

The First Period (1952-60) -- The bulk of Dick's short fiction and eight early novels. Dick as a fully professional, very competent and unremarkable author struggling, as the decade goes on, to break out of genre formulae and into his own, unique world. And in his view, failing -- the non-reception greeting his best work (and the apparent unpublishability of his non-science fiction) led him in 1960 to give up writing, and go to work in his third wife's jewelry store.[5] Published novels: **Solar Lottery** (1955), **The World Jones Made** (1956), **The Man Who Japed** (1956), **Eye in the Sky** (1957), **The Cosmic Puppets** (1957), **Time Out of Joint** (1959), **Vulcan's Hammer** (1960), **Dr. Futurity** (1960).

The Second Period (1962-65) -- The novel Dick wrote to

get out of working in the jewelry store, a novel largely set in a shop that becomes one, was the phenomenally sucessful **The Man in the High Castle,** written about and written using the **I Ching.** The **I Ching** recurs as the author of the tench's enigmatic slips of advice in **A Maze of Death** (and, symbolically, as the lying Book of Kalends in **Galactic Pot-Healer**). But it is the other Second Period novels, the imaginatively fecund, wildly plotted, and multiple charactered books Dick produced in a very short time that make the fullest use of **High Castle** elements: chance, fate, reality a fake, hatred of Germany, political satire as bitter and ironic as Brecht. Ten novels: **The Man in the High Castle** (1962), **The Game Players of Titan** (1963), **Clans of the Alphane Moon, The Penultimate Truth, The Simulacra, Martian Time-Slip, The Three Stigmata of Palmer Eldritch, The Unteleported Man** (all 1964), **Dr. Bloodmoney or How We Got Along After The Bomb** and **The Zap Gun** (both 1965). Important stories: "If There Were No Benny Cemoli" (1963), "Oh, to be a Blobel!," "Precious Artifact," "The Little Black Box" (1964), "Retreat Syndrome" (1965).

The Third Period (1966-76) -- In his introduction to the Gregg Press edition of **Counter-Clock World** David G. Hartwell suggests that one reason that all of Dick's novels since **Dr. Bloodmoney,** always excepting **Ubik,** are commonly thought "past-prime" by critics is that "SF fandom and SF criticism are generally ill-equipped to deal with metaphysics beyond the level of Arthur C. Clarke's evolutionary mysticism," as in **Childhood's End** (1953).[6] It is certainly true that Dick's unrecognized Third Period novels turn away from the bitter anti-Cold War satire of the Second Period (culminating in the bizarre self-parody of **The Zap Gun**) towards, finally, the expressed hope that help (an alien divinity) is on the way. This is just one difference. These novels gain a very sad, touching melancholy in their depictions of human relationships (particularly in the disintegrating marriages of **Now Wait for Last Year** and **Counter-Clock World**) only suggested in the earlier books, together with a corresponding gain in human nobility. The victims of the earlier novels (the ant-tankers in **The Penultimate Truth,** the Martian colonists of **Three Stigmata**) are passive targets for manipulation, while in **Now Wait for Last Year** or **Our Friends from Frolix 8** they are in open revolt. In the context of these touching, dynamic, metaphysical novels, the supposedly far superior **Ubik** seems a throwback to the nightmarish dream novels and collapsing realities of such earlier novels as **Eye in the Sky, Time Out of Joint,** and **The Three Stigmata of Palmer Eldritch.** Only now there's no wake-up call and death is final, not a dream. Nine novels are published through 1970: **Now Wait for Last Year** and **The Crack in Space** (1966), **Counter-Clock World** (1967), **The Ganymede Takeover** (written with Ray Nelson, 1967), **Do Androids Dream of Electric Sheep?** (1968), **Galactic Pot-Healer** and **Ubik** (1969), **A Maze of Death** and **Our Friends from Frolix 8** (1970).[7]

In 1970-73 Dick was afflicted with severe personal problems and did little writing. The books published before **A Scanner Darkly** (1977) were all essentially completed by the 1970 hiatus, though in fact Dick's Fourth Period can be said to begin with the story "A Little Something for Us Tempunauts" (1974), according to Dick his first story written after the break. (The controversial anti-abortion story "The Pre-Persons," also published in 1974, was according to Dick written some time earlier). For the record, the novels **We Can Build You** (1972), **Flow My Tears, the Policeman Said** (1974), and the collaboration with Roger Zelazny, **Deus Irae** (1976) can be considered as "Third Period" although even here there are problems. **We Can Build You** was first published as the serial "A.

Lincoln, Simulacrum" in 1969-70 (Dick says it dates ten years before that). **Deus Irae** was begun in 1964, turned over to Zelazny by 1968. **Flow My Tears** was essentially completed by 1970, and then set aside.

The Fourth Period (1977-82) -- **A Scanner Darkly** marks Dick's full emergence on the other side of the tragic, dramatic, yet finally artistically rewarding years of the early 1970s. **Scanner** is his brilliantly written memoir, hilarious in places and yet profoundly tragic, of his two years in the California Bay Area drug culture (1970-72), and attendant calamities.

His most recent novel, **VALIS** (1981), takes up the most important personal experience yet, the March 1974 "invasion of my my mind by a transcendentally rational mind... (a) divine power which was not evil, but benign...." [8] This of course parallels his vision of an evil deity in the sky of 1963, which bore the three stigmata soon given to Palmer Eldritch.

An author's personal life is irrelevant to his critics save where it affects his creative work. Dick's life over the past several years has been the explicit subject of his latest work, hence "admissable evidence." Yet between Dick's life and art, what matters is that **A Scanner Darkly,** and in its own way the strange and troubling **VALIS,** succeed on their own as realized works of art.

TWO: Dick's Heroes - Lost in the Maze

Most Dick commentators have noticed the seeming futility of Dick's protagonists against the horrors and amid the unreal realities they find themselves in. To Stanislaw Lem "the primary ontological elements - space and time - are Dick's instruments of torture" for those characters, [9] while Paul Williams is much more generous (and accurate):

> Dick's characters are all ultimately small (that is, ordinary, believable) people made big by their stamina

in the face of an uncertain world. Dick cares about the people in his books -- true, he contrives horrible things to happen to them, but that is in some sense beyond his control; he is like a god condemned to watch his universes fall apart as fast as he creates them, with his poor beloved characters trapped inside.[10]

Dick confirms his complete identification with his characters, and that the nightmares they suffer come from his own dreams. When he is writing "I am in the world I'm writing about. It is real to me, completely and utterly. Then, when I'm finished and have to stop, withdraw from that world forever -- that destroys me. The men and women have ceased talking. I'm alone."[11] Williams records that the stories of **Palmer Eldritch** and **A Scanner Darkly** were so frightening to him that he had difficulty reading the galleys for the printers.

There is a distinct progression in Dick's work from the conventional, standard science fiction heroes of the earliest work through the tormented "little men" of the middle period novels to the ultimate suffering protagonist, Dick himself, in **VALIS**. The phases of this progression match those of the novels.

The First Period includes Dick's earliest stories and novels. It is a critical commonplace that Dick's first novel, **Solar Lottery** (1955) marked a sharp rise in quality from, as Damon Knight put it, the "instantly saleable and instantly forgettable" stories he'd published in enormous quantity to that point.[12] Knight and others to the contrary, all but three of the early novels **(Eye in the Sky, The Cosmic Puppets, Time Out of Joint)** are fully anticipated in tone, texture, character, and plot structure by one or another another of the short stories. The worlds of oppressive bureaucracies, jerry-built dictatorships, Cold War crises, and mutated and pesky psi-powers that backdrop **Solar Lottery, The World**

Jones Made, The Man Who Japed, and **Vulcan's Hammer** are the same for long stories like "The Variable Man" (1953), "A World of Talent" (1954), and "The Minority Report" (1955). Some stories top these -- the grey ash post-Apocalypse parables "Second Variety" (1953) and "Captive Market" (1955) top all other stories in this genre, and are bleaker by far than Dick's later post-World War III world of mutants and "sports," **Dr. Bloodmoney** and **Deus Irae.** (The mutations in both were anticipated in "Planet for Transients," 1953). "The Golden Man" (1954), the perfect and all-powerful precog, anticipates in his awful isolation poor Manfred Steiner in **Martian Time-Slip.**

Dick's short fiction is inferior to his novels only in that the compressed space needed for the shorter format leaves so little room to weave the multi-character, loosely linked narrative webs that make the longer works so rich. It is significant that once Dick had mastered the multi-character, tangentially linked plot (first mastered in the non-science fiction **Confessions of a Crap Artist**) he wrote very little short work -- 19 stories since 1965, a number of them mere warm-ups for novels.

The two weakest First Period novels are **Vulcan's Hammer** and **Dr. Bloodmoney** (both 1960), expanded from earlier short stories ("Vulcan's Hammer," 1956, and "Time Pawn," 1954) to satisfy Ace paperback standards while he was concentrating on his mainstream novels. It is significant that Dick does his best work when ambitious -- the first novel, **Solar Lottery, is** markedly superior to most of his earlier short fiction, if only in first demonstrating the author's incredible facility in plot and character juggling, and in creating a believable "other world." **Solar Lottery** was written to break out of the short fiction field, **Confessions of a Crap Artist** to break into the "mainstream," **Time Out of Joint** to break into hardcover. Dick was proud when Ace Books editor Donald Wollheim denounced

Time Out of Joint and it was published as a hardcover mystery novel with a jacket making no references to Dick's other titles.[13]

All the published First Period novels, and most of the stories, feature single protagonists who can only be called heroes, placed in conflict with a society or event of distinct evil. Ted Benteley **(Solar Lottery),** Allen Purcell **(The Man Who Japed),** William Barris **(Vulcan's Hammer)** all begin idealistically serving an irrational society but end by rising against it. Security officer Cussick **(The World Jones Made)** is the first in a line of harassed Dick policemen holding the line against madness. The protagonists of **Eye in the Sky, The Cosmic Puppets, Time Out of Joint,** and **Dr. Futurity** all are at first baffled by the insane worlds they find themselves in, but once they figure out what's wrong they move forcefully to correct it. The partial exception here is Ragle Gumm in **Time Out of Joint,** whose lazy normalty is only gradually revealed to him as insane. He then behaves as heroically as the rest.

Confessions of a Crap Artist is a true transitional work here, none of its five major characters being heroic (or, in the case of the three people narrating the story, completely sane). The ten Second Period novels, with the exception of the weak novella **The Unteleported Man** (the second half of which was deleted by its publisher), all feature several marginally connected, marginally surviving characters trying to work out from under an oppressive society, often at cross-purposes.

Gone are the optimists of the early novels -- we now have protagonists who just scrape by. **Solar Lottery, The Man Who Japed, Time Out of Joint** all end with heroic vows and noble posing (the hero of **Japed** refusing safe passage from Earth in order to single-handedly face down the world government). No one in the Second Period is so foolish or idealistic, operating out of fear and instinct as much as courage. Witness Nicholas St. James, ant tanker in **The Penultimate Truth,** shaking with terror as he prepares to break through to the earth's surface, or Rachmael ben Applebaum in **The Unteleported Man,** driven to an insane eighteen year space flight by harranguing, sarcastic "creditor jet-balloons."

Dick had written of oppression before, rule by lies and dictatorial deception. The world of **Solar Lottery** was governed by a Quizmaster selected by chance who, once in absolute power, immediately became legal target for licensed assassins. Real power is held by great industrial combines, or "Hills." Floyd Jones **(The World Jones Made)** came to power through his precognitive ability to see one year into the future -- that, and his stirring up of hatred against harmless migrating alien "drifters." Morec (Moral Reclamation, in **The Man Who Japed**) ruled by gossip. The all-powerful **Vulcan's Hammer** was a self-perpetuating computer (like that in "Autofac," only meaner).

The evil of these worlds is minor compared to those of the Second Period. In **The Penultimate Truth** most of the world's population labors in "ant tanks" below the earth's surface, while a privileged few live on vast green estates (desmesnes), writing the propaganda sent below about the ever-raging nuclear war. In **The Unteleported Man** the overcrowded Earth's unemployed find useful work on a distant planet fifteen minutes away, one way only. Advertised as a paradise, it is in fact a slave state. (A similar device makes up **The Crack in Space**). Evil dominates the post-nuclear world of **Dr. Bloodmoney,** the Nazified planet of **The Man in the High Castle.**

The "vugs" who rule an occupied, depopulated Earth **(The Game Players of Titan)** lie to the few humans left about their prevention of human fertility. For their own sanity, the few humans left in "Precious Artifact" (1964) are comforted by their alien conquerors with artifical kittens and parrots. In "The Mold of Yancy" (1955), **The Penultimate Truth,** and **The Simulacra,** an unseen elite programs a fatherly robot president. In the latter novel, model after model is "married" to an eternally young and beautiful Jackie Kennedy figure. Germans, especially, are associated with the oppression: the German-led United Nations supports the one-way deportations of **The Unteleported Man,** Hermann Goering is brought in by time machine to **The Simulacra,** Nazi deception fuels **The Penultimate Truth,** Nazis rule with horrifying results in **The Man in the High Castle,** and in both **Dr. Bloodmoney** and **Deus Irae** (begun in 1964) World War III is touched off by a mad German scientist. The kicker is that Dick's last name, as revealed in **VALIS,** is German itself, meaning "Fat." [14]

The lies and mistruths of the Cold War era draw much of Dick's ire in this period. In this period the populace at large is gullible and passive. Just as in **The Penultimate Truth** there's no nuclear war, in **The Zap Gun** there's no Cold War, but power and profits are kept high by manufacturing and publicizing terror weapons like The Evolution Gun, The Psychic Conservation Beam, and The Garbage Can Banger. These are then "plowshared" into ridiculous consumer goods like ceramic owls. (Compare the phony plagues in **The Penultimate Truth** like "the Stink of Shrink." In more solemn, later work he gives us truly terrifying plagues, like the one in **Deus Irae** that causes organs to eat one another).

Satire and sarcasm give way in Dick's Third Period to sadness and sympathy, though minor works like **The Crack in Space** and **The Ganymede Takeover** are crowded, fairly comic throwbacks. (What can one make of Thisbe Olt's whore-in-the-sky Moments of Bliss satellite, with its breast-shaped landing field and winking pink nipple? The two headed George Walt in the same novel, **The Crack in**

Space, is a parody of Dick's other mutant villains, like Dr. Bloodmoney or Hoppy the phocomelus, Bloodmoney's downfall).

While in the Second Period Dick favored large, sprawling plots, with many characters, many of whom never met or heard of others, in the Third Period Dick cuts back to three or four important people instead of a dozen. Dick's prolific imagination narrows focus. If **The Simulacra** mixed Hermann Goering, a robot president, an ageless First Lady, an insane psychokinetic pianist, flying Nitz commercials that crawl into your car, a baroque jug band, and the "chuppers," Neanderthal throwbacks who see an opening in the future, or if **The Penultimate Truth** threw in the irrelevant pleasure of a time traveling scoop sent back to plant evidence of a non-existent battle between Indians and extra-terrestrials in the fossil record -- that was just the flood of Dick's genius at full tide.

Third Period Dick is simpler but deeper. In **Counter-Clock World,** universally regarded as "not working," Dick sketches an impossible universe where time is going backwards, the dead come to life, infants are absorbed into waiting wombs, excrement ("sogum") is proudly consumed and food is shamefacedly excreted into boxes of cornflakes and cans of peaches, to be sent back to the supermarket and ultimately planted in the ground.

Most if not all other science fiction writers would have dwelt on and further explained these miraculous happenings, dwelling on the time travel and other paradoxes, making the disturbing implications funny speculation (as Dick himself does, to a degree, in the story "Your Appointment Will Be Yesterday," 1966, featuring some of the same characters). Brian Aldiss, in his novel **An Age** (also known as **Cryptozoic,** 1967) brilliantly treats the same idea but ultimately, and disappointingly, passes it off as an insane fantasy.

Dick, instead, only casually deploys his backwards, or "Hobart Phase" world, being more interested in dovetailing into it the philosophy of Augustine and Erigena (a quotation from Erigena, "Love is the end and quiet cessation of the natural motion of all moving things, beyond which no motion continues," is the heading for Chapter Five). The novel in fact -- like much post-1965 Phil Dick -- is about love and the death of love, and its chief drama is not that of time reversal but the triangle of Sebastian Hermes, his wife Lotta, and Officer Joseph Tinbane.

Lotta and Tinbane are young, born as they were before the Hobart Phase took effect -- they never died and are actually getting younger. Hermes, however, owner of the Flask of Hermes Vitarium (which resurrects the old-born), is old-born himself, who still feels "on him, in the dreary part of the night, the coldness of the grave."[15]

Hermes loses Lotta to Tinbane through a failure of courage, wins her back after Tinbane's death by an act of fearful bravery that calls down the wrath of the forces raging above them. Hermes, Lotta, and Tinbane are all caught up in a battle of giants not that different from that which catches up the unhappily married couple of **Now Wait for Last Year,** or the policeman-android-wife triangle of **Do Androids Dream of Electric Sheep?** The antagonists in these battles are lesser evil vs. greater, the Anarch Peak's church against the Library **(Counter-Clock),** the rival alien forces of **Now Wait for Last Year.** While in Dick's earlier works one clearly evil side is presented as antagonist, here in Dick's Third Period his ordinary humans are being crushed by massive shades of grey, and must choose to help each other in order to stay alive.

In First Period Dick characters were secondary to the unfolding story, while in the Second Period they achieved a well judged balance with it. If the story was strong **(The Man in the High Castle)** so were the well-rounded, carefully created people in it; if the story was a helter-skelter patchwork **(The Simulacra),** so too were its colorful characters.

In Dick's Third Period he continued creating fictional worlds of greath depth and imaginative sadness (sadness more than mirth). The Earth of android animals and rampant decay ("kipple") of **Do Androids Dream** is as fully realized as the dreary Martian colonies of **The Three Stigmata of Palmer Eldritch** or **Martian Time-Slip** (with its decaying "gubble"). It is in the Third Period, however, that Dick's interest in his characters supercedes that in his story, in the Third Period where his empathy for his "poor beloved characters" comes through strongest.

It is in the fourth Period that Dick's hero becomes an anti-hero, becomes "himself." But this doesn't happen 'til after the author's most imaginative inhabitation of three seemingly unlikely protagonists, the "policemen trilogy" of **Do Androids Dream, Flow My Tears, the Policeman Said,** and **A Scanner Darkly.** Dick had used policeman protagonists before -- Cussick with his drug-taking wife in **The World Jones Made,** Tinbane with his helpless love for Lotta Hermes in **Counter-Clock World.** Given Dick's anti-establishment reputation (fully justified by the counter-authority parables of the Second Period, if not the liberal pieties of the First: the anti-McCarthyite message of **Eye in the Sky,** for example) it would seem strange he would extend his imaginative sympathy to the State's Enforcers.

Yet he does. The torn, muddled, tortured General Buckman (in **Flow My Tears,** arbiter of the fate of nominal leading man Jason Taverner) is in fact a General in the service of a dictatorial Amerika, a projection of a 1960s radical's most paranoid nightmare. The old college campuses are surrounded and the harried radicals live underground -- literally. But it is not merely an aching social conscience that spurs Buckman's tears, in a deservedly famous passage in Chapter Twenty-Seven ("A man, he thought, cries not for the future or the past but for the present.") It is his personal tragedies, a reflection of those of society but very much individualized nonetheless, that drive this gruff character and others like him to grief. For as Ruth Rae tells Taverner elsewhere in the novel: "Jason! Grief is the most powerful emotion a man or child or animal can feel. It's a good feeling."[16]

Rick Deckard in **Do Androids Dream,** Felix Buckman in **Flow My Tears,** Robert Arctor the narc in **A Scanner Darkly** are all policemen who learn how to grieve, following Officers Tinbane in **Counter-Clock World,** Cussick in **The World Jones Made,** characters in all walks of life in Dick's novels. Deckard needs a mechanical toad, Arctor a self-crucifixion with drugs. They share with other Dick characters, later Dick characters in particular, an ever widening capacity for grief. The ultimate product is "Horselover Fat," the Dick-figure in **VALIS,** who begins to question what empathy has brought him.

THREE: Dick's Themes - The Search for Caritas.

There are little themes, recurring phases, running motifs, in Dick's work, and big ones. Angry characters in book after book "grate" at each other. People fly in personal helicopters called "flapples" "flipflaps," "squibs," or "slivers." Sandra Miesel calls "modular building blocks" plot elements that are combined and recombined in each new Dick story, identifying them for **Eye in the Sky** as "commercial rivalries, employment crises, marital tensions, small group catastrophes, religious cults, and political menaces."[17]

I have pointed out many other recurring elements in the sections above. What is truly important, however, is the use to which Dick puts all these elements, all his imagination. An overarching world view emerges from careful study of Dick's work, all of it. This world view develops as his work does and is internally consistent even if frequently contradictory on the surface (the way, for example, aliens and **I Ching**-type books can be trusted in some novels but not in others).

To reduce this great body to a schematic diagram, we find that Dick is a fundamentally moralistic writer, with a strong belief in Good and Evil literally battling for men's souls, battling on the shifting, untrustworthy fields of an ever shifting "reality." On the one hand, and generally dominant, is Evil -- entropy, the Form Destroyer, the gubble god, the tomb world. On the other, struggling and never defeated, is Good -- the life-giving spirit, the restorative spirit, empathy, **caritas,** human caring. The lack of these things defines the Android. Thus:

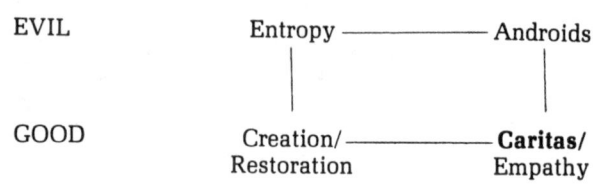

EVIL	Entropy	Androids
GOOD	Creation/Restoration	**Caritas/**Empathy

To flesh out this diagram all we need do is repair to virtually any of Dick's novels. From the First Period, for instance, Dick's one experiment in an almost Charles Williams-esque fantasy, **The Cosmic Puppets** (1957), literally incorporates the battle of Good and Evil in a small Virginia town, a boy who left there at age nine returning to find nothing as he'd left it. Everything is ersatz, shoddy - for the (ancient Zoroastrian) god "of darkness, filth and death, chaos and evil," Ahriman, has taken possession of half of the town. Ahriman rules in the person of a small boy who collects spiders, snakes, and rats, and who animates short-lived clay golems to carry out his raids. The other half of the town is held down for Good by a young girl, Mary, daughter of the town doctor. She has bees - a creative, building insect - on her side, and little else.

The returnee, Ted Barton, an insurance salesman, is drawn into a battle to restore the old town, to dissolve the false town built over the real one, using his own memories and those of one of the few townspeople who remembers the town before the Change: the town drunk, once a skilled engineer. It ultimately takes, however, the death and resurrection of Mary to restore the proper balance, which her sacrifice does by awakening Mary's father to his true status: that of a forgetful Ormazd, god of creation, a god who would rather not resume his true from. This plot turn takes **The Cosmic Puppets** out of a straight Williams-esque Christian allegory altogether, into something more daring and more Dickian.

The novel's richness, like so many of Dick's works, can only be suggested in this brief outline. The notion of the false town imposed on the real one, and the reluctance of the townspeople to resume their true identities, relate directly to the "insane" idea in **VALIS,** put forward by Dick in interviews as "maybe" his own belief, that the "real world" ended in the year 70, and that the intervening centuries of "spurious time" are "false memories" imposed on us.[18]

Ted Barton's employment as an insurance salesman relates to the humble small-scale capitalism of so many of Dick's characters, an array of jewelers (**The Man in the High Castle**), TV repairmen (**Dr. Bloodmoney**), and hustling businessmen (like Leo Bulero in **The Three Stigmata of Palmer Eldritch**). Running through all the books is a hatred for death, entropy, and decay (called "gubble" in **Martian Time-Slip,** "kipple" in **Do Androids Dream of Electric Sheep?**) on the one hand, and a love for the private concerns battling it on the other.

Manfred Steiner, the autistic boy of **Martian Time-Slip,** sees deeper into the "gubble" world of decay and entropy than others. He can see the future -- the universe decaying, and he with it. Another precog, the infallible Floyd Jones (**The World Jones Made**), is maddened by foreknowledge of his own death, and his decay afterwards. The half-alive of **Ubik** need "Ubik" in a spray-on can to restore what life they have.

Everywhere entropy. "Chickenhead" J.R. Isidore (namesake to the nominal author, the retarded science fiction collector, of **Confessions of a Crap Artist**), living in bombed over and "kippled" San Francisco in **Do Androids Dream of Electric Sheep?,** feels the presence of "the tomb world" -- had been there himself, "a pit of corpses and dead bones," where he had to stay "until the bones strewn around him grew back into living creatures." He had been sent there when his unique ability to restore dead animals to life (see **Counter-Clock World**) had been destroyed by the government. "The unique nodule which had formed in his brain" was destroyed by radioactive cobalt.[19]

Government crusades against special powers are found in Dick's writing as far back as "A World of Talent" (1954), where the talent in danger is that of a boy's to counteract the government's. Rule by those with special powers, whose psionic powers haven't been destroyed, forms a corrupt oligarchy in "A World of Talent" and in **Our Friends from Frolix 8.** Telepath wars rage in **Ubik** -- can't help the telepaths who are killed. Leo Bulero and others take "E-therapy" to advance their evolution in **The Three Stigmata of Palmer Eldritch,** but must look out that they don't regress instead. Special powers are no insurance against the temptations of power, or against universal decay.

What is a barrier is creation, or recreation -- to Dick, similarly blessed activities. The most masterful illustration of Dick's profound hope is the novel **Galactic Pot-Healer,** one of his finest. Joe Fernwright is Earth's best ceramics repairman, but in a world of thermoplastic, unbreakable pots he is sorely pressed for work. A world-wide welfare state keeps him fed and listless.

He is sent for by Glimmung, an ancient entity on Plowman's Planet, to raise the cathedral Heldscalla from the ocean floor where it has set decaying for several centuries. He is just one of many crafts-workers brought from all over the galaxy -- only to find that Glimmung, whimsically all-powerful on Earth (manifesting himself as hoops of fire and water behind a paisley shawl and the voice of a wind-up Victrola), is opposed by all the forces of the ocean tomb world.

Joe must fight himself and all logic to believe that the aging Glimmung can accomplish his miracle; Glimmung himself must battle his dark counterpart, an anti-Glimmung from an anti-cathedral. Finally Joe and the others from all planets are swallowed up by Glimmung (just as Old Mankind's champion Thors Provoni is literally a part of the great alien Morgo Rahn Wilc in **Our Friends From Frolix 8,** and the kindly empathetic telepathic Ganymedean slime mold Lord Running Clam saves Chuck Rittersdorf in **Clans of the Alphane Moon**).

The cathedral raised, Glimmung wants his partners to stay with him, inside of him, in fusion forever. But Joe wants out. Instead of repairing pots, he'll try making them - "his justification...for leaving Glimmung and all the others."[20]

He works hard on his maiden effort. "The pot was awful," is the book's final line, but Joe will try again, and again. Pots are in fact a running symbol, in Dick's work, for the finest of human qualities (though against this must be set the ceramic efforts of the awful Fay Hume in **Confessions of a Crap Artist).** Sweet Emily Hnatt (in **Three Stigmata,** regressed through E-therapy), and the one completely positive character in **Flow My Tears, the Policeman Said** , Mary Anne Dominic, both make pots. The pot Mary Anne gives Jason Taverner is the one thing that survives the novel's epilogue "openly and genuinely cherished. And loved," the fame of Jason Taverner and the police state of General Buckman both having died with time.

The pot Ho On appears to a pill-tripping Peter Sands **(Deus Irae)** as a giver of wisdom: "The little clay pot which came from the earth and can, like you, be smashed to bits and return to the earth, which lives only as long as your kind does." [21] The man-made sphere Orville, a plowshared weapon, gives similar religious counsel in **The Zap Gun.** In **VALIS** Horselover Fat's encounter with God, "the true God," not the "fucked-up blind deluded creator deity" who made the false world we're imprisoned in, comes through "the little pot Oh Ho which Stephanie had thrown for him on her kickwheel." [22]

* * * * *

Against the positive creativity of "special powers" and the craftsmanship (jewelry, pottery, salesmanship) of the individual, Dick sets the destructive powers of drugs, which as early in his work as **The World Jones Made** assume negative connotations (the drug-taking of Cussick's wife). Dick, unfairly, has an "acid-head" reputation.[23] Whatever the actual circumstances of his private life, in his creative work drugs were initially used to translate his characters to different realities, generally unpleasant ones. The Martian colonists in **The Three Stigmata of Palmer Eldritch** use Can-D to escape the tedium of their day-to-day lives, use Chew-Z for a bigger thrill and are trapped in Palmer Eldritch's head. The drug translations of **Now Wait for Last Year** are magical, addictive, and corrosive in increasing proportions.

By 1972 and his famous Vancouver speech, the drug addict assumes terrifying proportions as the android mind he has always hated, mental loss leaving "an insect intelligence:"

When a heroin addict confronts you, two insect eyes, two lightless slots of dim glass, without warmth or true life, calculate to the last decimal point how many tangible commodities you can be cashed in for. He, being already dead, views you as if you were already dead, or never lived.[24]

The eyes as "slots" exactly recall one of Palmer Eldritch's stigmata. Eldritch, in Dick's vision of him, is the God of Wrath, his fear that the universe is hostile to human love personified. For all that, Dick makes the Palmer Eldritch of his book a suffering and not too loathesome character. His great crime is not "personifying evil" but in trying to live forever through the absorption of other people's lives.

All these strands of Dick's work -- the drugs, the android people, the false reality, the question of God's benign or hateful face -- come together in **VALIS.** Perhaps it can be said that Dick has handled each question better before, individually, in other novels. **A Scanner Darkly** is the ultimate drug, or anti-drug, novel -- comic, pathetic, and genuinely horrifying as it laments the tragedy of "some people who were punished entirely too much for what they did. They wanted to have a good time, but they were like children playing in the street: they could see one after another of them being killed -- run over, maimed, destroyed -- but they continued to play anyhow." In his Author's Note to the novel (from which I quote) Dick makes clear how much of the story is autobiographical and lists fifteen of his friends who were destroyed in this way.

While **A Scanner Darkly** is elegiac, the first half of **VALIS** takes on a bitter, even self-pitying tone, between heavily footnoted bouts of philosophizing (in Chapter Three, for instance, we are hit with quotes from or references to **koine** Greek, two "minor" seventeenth century English metaphysical poets, Vaughn and Herbert, the role of the T-34 Soviet tank in World War II, Heraclitus, Daedalus, Parsifal, and the nature of time). Horselover Fat, Dick's perplexed alternate ego, debates the reality of his visions with himself and his skeptical friends (who include a science fiction novelist named Philip K. Dick).

The second half of **VALIS** takes off when Fat discovers that his speculations about the good "homoplasmates" (perfect human beings such as Jesus and Buddha) trying to help mankind may actually be true and that VALIS (Vast Active Living Intelligence System) is speaking to him and to others. He makes the connection through a science fiction rock musical movie by that name, and for awhile -- with both Dick and Fat meeting the baby who is VALIS personified -- things seem to be working out well. Philip K. Dick and Horselover Fat merge into one soul; but entropy wins another round when the baby dies in a freak accident. The book ends with Horselover Fat returned and watching television, searching for a new message from VALIS above. Still searching for **caritas.**

Never, do I think, has a writer so laid himself on the line as Philip K. Dick does in **VALIS.** Throughout his career Dick has been concerned with his reputation, of not appearing as deluded or as a drug addict.[25] Yet knowing full well that some who would read **VALIS** would react by deeming him crazy, he went ahead anyway (and, in terms of reputation in certain circles, paid the full price).[26] What price the search for **caritas?** A price Dick feels is worth it.

* * * * *

Dick's search for **caritas** begins with his aversion to androids, the insect brain, the mind without pity. Cold, heartless people reoccur like specters in his work: the universe of Palmer Eldritches his drug takers find themselves in; Fay Hume in **Confessions of a Crap Artist** driving her husband to his death; Pat Conley in **Ubik** laughing and mocking as a dying Joe Chip mounts the endless stair to his room.

Sometimes, often, the android folk are not deliberately malicious. They are schizoid, isolated in themselves. There is little difference between Pris the maker of androids in **We Can Build You** (her "Abraham Lincoln" simulacrum is warmer hearted) and "Pris" the genuine android of **Do Androids Dream of Electric Sheep?**, who kills Rick Deckard's real sheep and helps torture J.R. Isidore's live insect. Yet Louis Frauenzimmer (**We Can Build You**), Rick Deckard and Isidore are all in love with Pris. This too is not uncommon.

Dick does not hate his humanoid machines -- in fact, the cranky automobiles that debate their drivers (**The Game Players of Titan**) and the robot who is studying to be a freelance writer (**Galactic Pot Healer**) are some of his books' most endearing characters. (On the other hand look out for the flying Nitz commercials, floating creditor jet-balloons, and taxis that betray you to the police despite being bribed -- this last in **Now Wait for Last Year.** Or the infuriating doors that want money to open, in **Ubik**). What Dick hates are people who act like machines. These are the people who have only their private worlds (the **idios kosmos**) and not a shared world with others (the **koinos kosmos**).

> In all my works, well, virtually all, the protagonist is suffering from a breakdown of his **idios kosmos** -- at least we hope that's what's breaking down, not the **koinos kosmos**. As his **idios kosmos** breaks down, the objective shared universe emerges more clearly... but it may be quite different from the **idios kosmos** which he is in the process of losing. Hence, strange transformations take place....[27]

Thus the bizarre worlds of **Eye in the Sky, The Cosmic Puppets, Time Out of Joint, The Three Stigmata of**

Palmer Eldritch, Martian Time-Slip, Now Wait for Last Year, Ubik and **A Maze of Death** that most Dick commentary has tried to puzzle out. Frequently, what seems unreal (the soft drink stand that dissolves in **Time Out of Joint,** leaving a piece of paper saying "Soft Drink Stand") is what's actually true. The crowded, smoky, noisy San Francisco Mr. Tagomi finds himself in after staring at the piece of jewelry full of **wu,** in **The Man in the High Castle,** is the real San Francisco, in the world where the Nazis lost. The **I Ching,** through Hawthorne Abendsen, has written **The Grasshopper Lies Heavy** in that book to tell the world that the Nazis never could have won.

To do battle against entropy -- the fakery of Ahriman's false town in **The Cosmic Puppets,** the mass produced antiques collected in **The Man in the High Castle,** the phony half-life decay of **Ubik** -- stand struggling entrepreneurs and artisans. The town drunk has his laboriously made Spell Remover. Frank Frink stops making fake Civil War guns, starts creating jewelry with **wu.** Robert Childan stops selling those guns, and with great shame and difficulty spurns an offer to mass produce Frink's jewelry as good luck trinkets. (Tagomi uses one of those guns to kill a Nazi thug).

Dick sees these figures as "redeemers... the minor man asserts himself in all his hasty, sweaty strength. In the ruins of Earth's cities he is busily constructing a little factory that turns out cigars or maps...."[28]

One of Dick's redeemers is Leo Bulero, Can-D drug pusher, big-talking businessman, who nonetheless is the man who stops Palmer Eldritch. His "inter-office audio-memo circulated to Pre-Fash level consultants at Perky Pat Layouts, Inc., ...immediately upon his return from Mars," printed as frontispiece to **The Three Stigmata,** is what Dick has called "my credo -- all I actually have to say or want ever to say," adding darkly that it was deleted from the German edition.[29]

> I mean, after all; you have to consider we're only made out of dust. That's admittedly not much to go on and we shouldn't forget that. But even considering, I mean it's a sort of bad beginning, we're not doing too bad. So I personally have faith that even in this lousy situation we're faced with we can make it. You get me?[30]

Against the dust -- **caritas,** love. If **VALIS** shows the pain empathy has brought Dick, the totality of his work shows the need for empathy. Between the self-snuffing robot of "The Electric Ant" (1969), who slices apart his reality tape and witnesses the disappearance of the world, and the pain-grasping empathy boxes of "The Little Black Box" (1964) and **Do Androids Dream,** lies the richness, depth, and greatness of Philip K. Dick's vision.

> Throughout...the theme of fakes, of deception, the theme of guile and cunning, are evident, but I would also like to have a theme of human trust noted, even though it may be submerged at times under the ominous....**Caritas** in the final analysis is emotional trust. I trust, then, that you will not misread me and see dislike and anger only; please reach out to me at the core below that, the core of love.[31]

* * * * *

FOUR: Postscript (1984)

The Divine Invasion (1981) and the posthumously published **The Transmigration of Timothy Archer** (1982) round off Dick's career, his Fourth period, and his life, all too neatly. Already these last two novels have been joined with **VALIS** to form a "gnostic trilogy" or "VALIS trilogy."[32] To me **The Divine Invasion** was a complete success (after the incredible density of **VALIS,** lucid and direct). It was at once a sequel to the earlier book and an answer to it, for while **VALIS** is a work of mitigated despair **The Divine Invasion** is probably the most optimistic volume in Dick's canon. Evil is defeated, Good victorious, with Good defined yet again as people helping and caring for each other -- "mutuality," or **caritas** in action.

In **The Divine Invasion** -- Dick's last science fiction novel, **Timothy Archer** being straight fiction -- the pattern of Dick's recurring themes makes one more appearance. We have multiple realities, with Herb Asher's transition from dream state (on his dome on a distant planet, and later from cryonic suspension) to living reality, and also the transition from an Earth governed by a Catholic-Communist world state to a happier world half-way through the book. The political satire recalls the Second Period, the urgency of the change of regime **Now Wait for Last Year.**

That the latest incarnation of VALIS on Earth is born brain-damaged should not surprise the reader of, say, **Dr. Bloodmoney,** in which Earth's salvation comes from a small girl's unborn twin brother, or anyone who recalls the literally "special" status of "chickenhead" Jack Isidore **(Do Androids Dream)** or the saintly hebephrenics in **Clans of the Alphane moon.** The characters of Zina, Rybys, and Linda Fox are strong, positive female characters answering the more negative women, associated with drugs or death, of such other late novels as **We Can Build You, Flow My Tears, A Scanner Darkly,** and the willfully dying Sherri in **VALIS.** (Also very positive, of course, is Angel Archer in **Transmigration**).[33]

Evil in **The Divine Invasion** is seen to be the entropic sluggishness Herb Asher and Rybys Romney (lazy, sloppy, selfish) are both trapped in initially. In goat form Belial (Evil, The Accuser) late in the book is able to assault Linda Fox. Continuing a career-long linkage of high human art and what is Good, and commercial mediocrity with what is

Bad, Dick here has Good signal itself with Mahler, John Dowland, and Linda Fox's voice, while Evil is associated with soupy elevator music versions of "Fidder on the Roof" and "South Pacific."

Finally, and most beautifully, we have the resolution of Dick's career-long ballet of policemen on the brink of becoming androids even as they fight them. Late in the novel Herb Asher is on his way to visit Linda Fox in Hollywood. He has met her through the stereo business run by himself and the Prophet Elijah, another pair of small businessmen in the Dick tradition, like the team of Louis Frauenzimmer and Abraham Lincoln in **We Can Build You.** Suddenly Herb's car fills full of elevator music (just as he spent ten years listening to in cryonic suspension). A robot-like policeman pulls Herb over, his face covered with a plastic mask "resembling a World War I fortification" (and also Palmer Eldritch).[34] With great difficulty Herb is able to convince the policeman that he, Herb Asher, could indeed be the "legal father of God," and that the outcome of a crucial battle between Good and Evil could indeed depend on his joining Linda Fox in Hollywood. Herb tells the policeman:

> "...I see some response in you, some amount of human warmth."
>
> "I am not a machine," the cop said.[35]

As he lets him go, the policeman asks Herb Asher to pray for him.

* * * * *

For all the power of its ending, its willed epiphany of Archer's redemption, **The Transmigration of Timothy Archer** struck this reader as being somewhat limited by the author's holding back of his imaginative powers, writing as he was a straight literary novel that was moreover about deceased friends of his. What comes through very strongly, besides the **"caritas**-at-last" message of the book (in his last two books Phil indeed seemed to have found what he'd been looking for all of his life) is the author's great skill at relating naturalistic character and behavior. Never absent from his work, going back to stretches of the earliest stories and novels (and particularly strong, of course, in the literary novels written in the 1950s), Dick's gift for portrayed realism came on very strongly indeed in his Fourth Period, **Flow My Tears, the Policeman Said** (last of the Third Period works) being the last Dick novel to have any sense of strain in the characterization or dialogue (in this case, with the book's various predatory females).

A Scanner Darkly and **VALIS,** inbetween the sordid or incredible happenings, are brilliantly realized as novels of character and dialogue. And it is these strengths -- despite a disappointing handling of Bishop Archer himself, the original model for the character perhaps being too powerful for Dick to capture in print and not overpower his thesis -- that ultimately carry **The Transmigration of Timothy Archer** through to its triumphant conclusion. Above all else, the realization of the character of Angel Archer fulfills the claims Dick makes for her in this volume: she is magnificent.

* * * * *

At the conclusion of a late-1981 supplement to my original essay (covering **The Divine Invasion** only), I predicted that Dick's two novels then under way, **Timothy Archer** and **The Owl by Daylight,** could be the beginning of a new cycle (a "Fifth Period") for their author. We shall never know, but it does seem to be now that Philip K. Dick did continue to grow as an artist -- to continually transform himself into something eternally fresh, even as he continued to grapple with the same old eternal questions --

right to the end of his life.

It is my hope that my interviews with Phil Dick will be taken as something of a great author's last testament, a commentary on his work he never had the time to write, but took the time to say. It is in this spirit, as the amanuensis to a great man, that I present **Philip K. Dick: In His Own Words.**

* * * * *

FIVE: Comment - by Philip K. Dick

(For whatever it's worth, and to me it's worth a great deal, Phil Dick had this to say about my theories on his writing, expressed during our first interview session in April 1981):

PKD: I really felt (reading your piece) that for the first time I saw an organic evolution in my writing that no one had ever spotted before. There was a logic in the transformations from one period of my writing to the next. And in four periods is the correct division, not three, which is the conventional division of my writing, into three periods. The early stuff, which is journeyman apprentice stuff -- then the middle period, which is the glorious flowering of a great talent -- and then the degenerate mystical crap of the last period.

Well, I'm a little tired of reading that, because it doesn't give me much motivation to write. But your four divisions, in which each one surmounts the previous one, is I think accurate, and secondly, it also is encouragement to me to procede. For one thing, you find out as I recall that one of the great, basic evolutionary elements is that of characterization. In each period there's more emphasis on character.

Now to be quite honest, this has helped me in framing this new novel that I'm working on now **(The Transmigration of Timothy Archer).** It's obvious that whether I designed it this way deliberately it's still going to come out anyway that I'm going to emphasize character even more than I've emphasized it before, based on the logic that you find in those four periods. Even if I don't know that I'm going to do this, this is going to happen. Character will predominate now, enormously.

So that was very useful to me in approaching this contemporary novel I'm writing...The thing is, after reading your article, I can see that if I wanted to emphasize something other than character I really have no power to do that, because the logic of the former works is always in me. I really try to supercede each previous work.

Like, I wrote **Scanner** continually thinking about **Flow My Tears,** that I had to top that. And likewise with **VALIS.**

GR: Not so much topping, as building on. Each work builds on the preceding one. You know, I wrote it as a labor of love, 'cause my jaw dropped when I read some of the stuff that had been written about you, this alleged "decline."

PKD: You see, that particular prejudice that they have doesn't given me any incentive for going on, because as far as they're concerned I haven't done anything good (since 1965).

It's a formula feeling that critics have agreed on, from reading one another. They read one another's writing, you see. And this is the stock view of my writing. Darko Suvin is the one who expresses it most succinctly...which I don't want to hear. That's not what I want to hear.

* * * * *

Notes for "Philip K. Dick and the Search for Caritas"

(1) Philip K. Dick, "Introduction," **The Golden Man.**
(2) John Brunner, "The Work of Philip K. Dick," **New Worlds,** No. 166 (September 1966), p. 143.
(3) Stanislaw Lem, "Science Fiction -- A Hopeless Case: With Exceptions" (1972), in Bruce Gillespie, ed. **Philip K. Dick: Electric Shepherd,** p. 79.
(4) At the time of writing this, the major Dick criticism which has appeared since his death was not yet available, and I was working with the meager, picayune Gillespie and George Turner efforts in Gillespie's anthology, and such pieces as Darko Suvin's "Artifice as Refuge and World View: Philip K. Dick's Foci" **(Science-Fiction Studies** 5, 1975, later reprinted in the Olander-Greenberg anthology **Philip K. Dick, 1983).** Dick took strong exception to this piece -- see Chapter 11 of this book. For the record, I discovered Suvin's division of Dick's career into three periods after developing my own four-period scheme, but before writing my essay.
(5) Paul Williams, "Introduction," **Confessions of a Crap Artist.** I am following Angus Taylor's lead in his monograph **Philip K. Dick and the Umbrella of Light** by not paginating quotes from specific editions of Phil's books, as they exist in so many editions.
(6) David G. Hartwell, "Introduction," **Counter-Clock World** (Boston: Gregg Press, 1979).
(7) As I would learn from my conversations with Phil, **The Crack in Space** is a work of the Second Period held up and printed later.
(8) This chronology was pieced together from Phil's own published articles, interviews, and letters. The quote concerning the 1974 vision is from the Charles Platt interview, **Dream Makers** (New York: Berkley Books, 1980), pp. 154-55.
(9) Lem, Gillespie **op. cit.,** p. 80.
(10) Paul Williams, "The Three Stories of Philip K. Dick," **Rolling Stone,** November 6, 1975, p. 46.
(11) **ibid.,** p. 94.
(12) Damon Knight, **In Search of Wonder** (Chicago: Advent Publishers, 2nd ed., 1967), p. 228. Dick published an incredible 111 short stories in 1952-59, sixty-two in the pre-**Solar Lottery** years of 1952-54. Thereafter production tapers off rapidly. See the year-by-year story production chart in Daniel J.H. Levack's **PKD: A Philip K. Dick Bibliography,** pp. 142-45.
(13) Lou Stathis, "Introduction," **Time Out of Joint** (Boston: Gregg Press, 1979).
(14) Dick's ancestry was Scotch-Irish. "Horselover" in **VALIS** is Greek for Philip, "Fat" German for Dick.
(15) **Counter-Clock World,** chapter one.
(16) **Flow My Tears, The Policeman Said,** chapter eleven.

42 : PHILIP K. DICK

(17) Sandra Miesel, "Introduction," **Eye in the Sky** (Boston: Gregg Press, 1979), p. vi.
(18) Daniel DePres, "An Interview with Philip K. Dick," **Science Fiction Review** 19 (August 1976), p. 11.
(19) **Do Androids Dream of Electric Sheep?**, chapter two.
(20) **Galactic Pot-Healer**, chapter sixteen.
(21) **Deus Irae**, chapter three.
(22) **VALIS**, chapter five. I once had Phil show me the actual Oh Ho, a beautiful little blue pot, which he kept carefully hidden away. It had actually been made for him as described in **VALIS.**
(23) See Chapter 1 of this book. Also, the Williams interview in **Rolling Stone** and the Arthur Byron Cover interview in **Vertex** (February 1974) go into this question in some detail.
(24) Letter of Introduction, "The Android and the Human," Gillespie, **op. cit.**, p. 50.
(25) Dick was quite upset when Harlan Ellison's introduction to his story, "Faith of Our Fathers," in the anthology **Dangerous Visions** (1967) implied that he'd written it, and also **The Three Stigmata**, under the influence of LSD. Yet in the 1974 **Vertex** interview (**op. cit.**, p. 96) he told Cover that he had written blurbs for himself saying "He (Dick) has been experimenting with hallucinogenic drugs to find the unchanging reality beneath our delusions." Also in 1967, according to the file of letters at Cal State Fullerton, he forced an apology from a fan who had linked his name with a report about brain damage from amphetamines. By the 1974-75 interviews with Williams and Cover he was out in the open about his drug use, and by **VALIS** in 1981 out in the open about everything else.
(26) See the Ursula LeGuin material in this book, Chapter 15.
(27) Dick, letter of June 8, 1969, Gillespie, **op. cit.**, p. 32
(28) Dick, letter of September 9, 1970, **ibid.**, p. 45.
(29) Dick, "The Android of the Human," **ibid.**, p. 66
(30) Frontispiece, **The Three Stigmata of Palmer Eldritch**. Also quoted directly by Dick, **ibid.**, p. 66
(31) Dick, "Afterword," **The Golden Man.**
(32) See for example Robert Gilbreath's "Redemption and Doubt in Philip K. Dick's **VALIS** trilogy," **Extrapolation**, Vol. 24 No. 2 (Summer 1983), p. 108.
(34) The full significance of the recurring image of the World War I fortification mask in Dick's work relates to the stories Dick's father told him of his participation in that war. See the second volume of this series.
(35) **The Divine Invasion**, chapter eighteen.

* * * * *

PART TWO
In His Own Words:
Writing Science Fiction

CHAPTER 3
Why Science Fiction?
The Benign Gods
Moral Choices

10-12-81

GR: Why do you like writing science fiction?
PKD: Because it gives me a chance to be crazy and be paid for it. I can write real weird stuff about real weird people doing real weird things where people walk through walls, like Christ did at the end of the Gospels. And give some sort of pseudo-scientific explanation for it, like they're all dead.

Can't do that in a mainstream novel.

I can play with the universe like it's silly putty. Somebody in a letter once said that Phil Dick's universe is made of silly putty, and that perfectly sums it up. I love to just play games with time-space causality. It's my old interest in epistemology. For one thing I don't really believe the universe is real, I don't believe we're sitting here. I think we're brains yoked in tandem and we're being fed sensory-sight stimulation directly to the brain. And they're writing down how we respond to various problems that arise.
GR: Who are they?
PKD: Well I guess the gods. They're good, they're benign. If they weren't benign they would have executed us a long time ago, as (Abraham) Maslow says. But we're being tested. And we're being tested in very small matters. It's not the big decisions that we're being tested regarding. Because there we know we're being tested, we sense that. We sense moral elements. It's situations that are so small that we don't even sense there's a moral element involved. I really believe this very firmly, I'm convinced of it. The real test comes where you're not even conscious that there is a moral element in the decision. You can see this in other people.

A friend of mine was once telling me about a cat that they took way out in the country to get rid of, and dumped seven miles from town. A week later it shows up with the pads all worn off its feet, it walked all the way back. And I said, where is the cat now? and she says Oh, we had it killed. The fact that she'd done something **terrible** didn't even occur to her. You see, I feel we're being tested, all of us.

Where we don't see any moral element is where the test comes. If we see a moral element, we will probably make a deliberate choice. It's those little unconscious choices.

I'll give you an example that occurs to me now. I was at the supermarket last week, real late, buying a bunch of junk food for myself. And there was a guy ahead of me buying a can of beer. It wasn't an old guy, he was kind of heavy set, burly guy in his thirties. And he was drunk. And he didn't have enough money for the can of beer. And without even thinking about it I tossed him a quarter, but it wasn't enough. I thought he was only a dime short, but he wasn't even close. Poor guy, not even close. He was so drunk. I had to deal with the checker as to how much was needed. And he was moved, although admittedly he was very drunk, he was moved to incredible emotion. He came back, told me his name, shook hands with me, said it meant a lot to have somebody do that for him. Sure hope he wasn't driving.

That's what we're going to find scored. They're going to shoot back on the screen replays of those things, where we didn't see the moral issue involved.

So in a sense what I'm really saying is that all life is a moral issue. Which is a very Jewish idea. The Hebrew idea about God is that God is found in morality, not in epistemology. That is where the Almighty exists, in the moral area. It isn't just what I said once, that in Hebrew monotheism ethics devolve directly from God. That's not it. It's that God and ethics are so interwoven (that) where you have one you have the other.

I think that in a sense that is my belief, yes, I do believe this honestly. I will not be scored, you will not be scored, for being smart. We will not be scored on anything that works for our survival. The payoff on that is survival. And smart ultimately means doing the thing that you're going to survive better...

* * * * *

CHAPTER 4
Caritas / A Beetle In Third Grade / Cockroaches Are An Exception / Seeing Things Five Different Ways

4-22-81

GR: How did the concept of **caritas** first present itself to you? That our salvation is in helping each other?
PKD: I really think -- I've thought about this -- and it goes back to an incident when I was in the third grade, where I was tormenting a beetle. It was taking refuge in an empty snail shell. He'd come out of the snail shell and I'd mash at

him with a rock, and he'd run back into the snail shell. I'd just wait 'til he'd come out.

And he came out, and all of a sudden I realized -- it was total **satori,** just infinite, that this beetle was like I was. There was an understanding. He wanted to live just like I was, and I was hurting him. For a moment -- it was like Siddhartha does, like was that dead jackal in the ditch -- I was that beetle. Immediately I was different. I was never the same again. I was totally aware of what I was doing, I was just transformed -- my essence was changed.

It was like when Plato describes remembering the form, recovering the knowledge of the forms. It was a complete understanding of the life and aspirations of that beetle, and the importance of his life. His life was as precious to him as my life was to me. I've never lost that.

I make no distinctions between creatures and humans, and animals and bugs. A bug's life is as precious as my life is to me. Because all life is God.

Cockroaches are the exception. I was telling all this to Charles Platt and I was mentioning how I'd killed a cockroach, and he was just shocked. And I said, well I don't really include wasps and cockroaches.

GR: Because?

PKD: Because I don't like them. And he says, well that violates your very premise. And I say, yes, and I'm going to keep doing it. I said, what I love to do is cut a cockroach in half and watch the two halves crawl away in different directions. And he just turned pale.

And I say, Charles, that just shows how far I've led you on my empathy trip, that you would turn pale at the thought of me killing a cockroach.

GR: I suffered a lot when I moved up to San Francisco, and had to start eliminating cockroaches. I'd always let trapped flies out of window screens, and carried spiders outdoors, but when I got up there and they were crawling out of my bread, I began killing them.

PKD: Take refuge in Zoroaster's contention that bugs like that were made by Ahriman (the evil god of destruction in Zoroasterism and in **The Cosmic Puppets**). And not by Ormazd. They are part of a different domain.

GR: Good enough. I like that.

PKD: Flies and excrement and dirt, he says, were made by Ahriman.

I went from that beetle on to a further series of revelations which finally became excruciating. You mention in your article, that **VALIS** shows the price of empathy, but the body of the writing, the corpus, shows the necesity. That was one of the most marvelous statements I'd ever read...

Your analysis of my writing is of it as an organically building evolutionary process, and your article is the same way....First you analyze and then you synthesize....Some people can analyze and some people can synthesize. I can't analyze. I can synthesize real good but I can't analyze. I have no analytical powers whatsoever.

I can put things together. But I depend on what Jung calls my intuitive faculty, my gestalting factor. For instance, I cannot analyze my own writing, even though I've written it. In no way can I analyze it. If people ask me what one of my novels is about I can't tell them a thing.

My faculty, the faculty I use, is that I can look at the same thing five different ways. I can look at the same cluster of things and see five different ways they can link together. They can add up to five different wholes. (Phil was famous for having several different ways of seeing the same event, as for instance the 1971 break-in at his house, which he analyzed several different ways in the Paul Williams **Rolling Stone** interview, or the VALIS events).

* * * * *

CHAPTER 5
Christian Beliefs / The Fallen World / C.S. Lewis / Charles Williams / Olaf Stapleton Benign Conspiracies / Tolkien

4-22-81

GR: You're familiar with the Christian belief, that God created the Earth and it was good, but Man fell, Lucifer - evil - took over, and the Earth is now under enemy occupation. The Earth is quarantined, but God breaks periodically through the screen, put up by the enemy, who controls earth.

PKD: That's the whole premise for **The Divine Invasion.** I adopt that premise entirely. I'm familiar with the premise, it's your standard fallen world. It's an adversary situation.

I've never heard it expressed so coherently, I find it a very formidable statement now that I've heard somebody say it in a reasonable way. Usually they just dilate forever on these obscure points, but you've phrased it beautifully. Let me think, 'cause I did write a book about that, my last book. Shit! (laughs).
GR: Have you read C.S. Lewis? That's where I got it from.
PKD: Well it's funny, no I haven't, and the funny thing is that John Clute in reviewing **The Divine Invasion** mentioned that it's so much like C.S. Lewis that essentially it's saying the same.

(Phil went on to say that he had read a couple of Lewis' books and **That Hideous Strength** "is sitting over there, recommended by a Catholic friend." Asking him about other favorite science fiction and fantasy authors of mine, I found that he didn't know Charles Williams at all, whose novels of everyday life shading into the supernatural I was very fond of. I had compared **The Cosmic Puppets** with a Williams novel in my essay. I told him Williams was associated with Lewis, Tolkien, and the other Oxford Christians).
PKD: Do you suppose that I have independently rediscovered theism? Thinking to myself, in my artless fashion, that I had stumbled onto a major new concept, and all I'm doing is reinventing traditional orthodox Christianity?
GR: It's the same question as did Van Vogt create **Slan,** or had he read Olaf Stapleton first? Do you like Stapleton?
PKD: Very much. **Last and First Man** (1930), I think it's one of the greatest books ever written.
GR: To me that was it for a long time, in terms of science fiction.
PKD: That is so good, that if you were a science fiction

writer starting out, you can give up at that point. You can say, this is the epitome of great science fiction. You can't exceed the expanse of his imagination. It's **incredible.**

He was really great. I'll tell you another book I liked, it was **The Man Who Was Thursday** (G.K. Chesterson, 1908).

GR: That's a real Phil Dick reality trip -- everyone turns out to be a member of the same conspiracy.

PKD: That's a lot of fun. I know Robert Anton Wilson, and we both love conspiracy. We don't love it in the sense of -- the normal conspiracy buff, who's convinced that there's all these demonic and malignant conspiracies to enslave mankind. An example is (William S.) Burroughs' conviction about the parasitic information virus which has afflicted our minds and made us all stupid. They've taken over the planet. That's cool.

Bob Wilson and I have this conviction that there are benign conspiraces going on, which is kind of interesting psychologically. You can see the psychological dynamism going on, in the conviction of an evil conspiracy, a paranoid thing. But it's very hard to figure out what's going on if you love the idea that the world is secretly ruled by very benign people, who are promoting health, happiness, and prosperity for all. What's the psychological roots of that? Just naivete! (laughs).

* * * * *

GR: I notice you make a couple of references to Tolkien in your work. (In **A Maze of Death, The Lord of the Rings** saga is a revered classic; Ben Tallchief plays a 3-D visrecord of it and confronts a Gandalf who seems to address him. Tallchief considers him "a mythological character who probably never existed").

PKD: That was really before the Tolkien cult started. I saw the cult coming. I read the books when they came out, the

English editions before they were available in America. (This would be in 1955-56). I had read **The Hobbit** (1938) when I was a child; it had come out and I read it as a child. And I really loved it.

Of course now I know he based a lot of it on (Wagner's) "The Ring," "The Ring of the Nibelungen." The curse of the ring, the power of the ring.

* * * * *

CHAPTER 6
Earliest Writing / "I Love To Write" / Charybdis / Borges, Flaubert, Beethoven / Idioms

4-22-81

GR: How did you get into writing?
PKD: My mother was a writer, or she wanted to become a published writer. She used to write novels and short stories. She sold one short story once, to a little throwaway magazine called **Family Circle.** She sold it for 40 bucks. That's all she ever sold. But I got the idea that writing was very important.

I wrote my first novel when I was 13. I taught myself to touch type when I was in junior high, or grammar school. Sixth or seventh grade, I taught myself to touch type, from her book, which she had used in a course on typing. Took the book, learned to type. Wrote a novel, called **Return to Lilliput.** Wasn't very good.

GR: Based on Swift?

PKD: Loosely based on Swift. Had a lot of submarines in it.

GR: Since then, what have been your writing habits? do you get a lot of satisfaction from it? Is it something you like to do -- something you can't help?

PKD: (laughs) "Can't help." Wind me up and I go to the typewriter.

It's normal for me to write. It's as normal for me to write as it is for some people to eat peanuts. Or go to the movies. Or take a drive in the country. Writing is -- I carry my clipboard with me, all around the apartment. I'm always and forever taking notes. I love to write. If I'm not working on a thing to be published, I just work on notes. I just take endless notes. Mostly philosophical notes. For instance I'll research a philosopher, and I'll spend weeks making comments on him. Just sitting there doing it. Can't sell notes, you know. Got a stack, 600,000 words of notes.

It gets you fluent, where you can express your thoughts in written words. It's very important to be able to do that. It's wonderful. Not a waste of time.

And as you read -- reading is the other side of that, is constantly reading. You catch turns of phrases that people use. I was reading this article on philosophy, and he says Hume believes such-and-such, and Locke believes he knows not what. What a wonderful turn of phrase!

I came across a paragraph in the Britannica the other day, which I read to Paul (Williams) the other night. I thought it one of the most amusing paragraphs I'd ever read and it's not supposed to be funny at all. It's in a reference work. It's talking about Scylla and Charybdis, the two threats (in Greek mythology) on either side of the straight. If you veer to the left, you veer into Scylla. If you veer to the right, Charybdis. The expression, "between Scylla and Charybdis" means you're damned if you do and damned if you don't.

So they're talking about Charybdis and it says "Charybdis, who lurked under a fig tree, a bow shot away on the opposite shore, drank down and belched forth the ocean twice a day, and was fatal to shipping." (laughs). I would say I would think so! Belching forth the entire Mediterranean twice a day would certainly make her fatal to shipping!

Now you see like I read that, and I admire the fact that in that one sentence he's presented, or she's presented, everything you'd want to know about Charybdis. I now have a complete conception of Charybdis in my mind, on the basis of that marvelous and terse sentence. She was "fatal to shipping." Nothing more need be said about Charybdis. We now know exactly what these guys encountered when they encountered Charybdis. -- She was actually a whirlpool.

So I'm reading, writing. I've been reading (Jorge Luis) Borges (the Argentine fantastist). Paul sent me Borges.

I'm not like you, when you said you like a writer you read everything he wrote (which is what I'd told Phil about my discovery of him). I've had the idea I've read Borges, and I've read one book.

GR: Well, I have the idea I've read Flaubert and I've read one book.
PKD: I'll bet you read **Madame Bovary.**
GR: Yeah.
PKD: Flaubert probably had some other book he liked, and people didn't read it.

GR: Yes, he did! **Bouvard and Pecuchet,** which nobody would read. It's about these guys who collect a great dictionary of misinformation.

PKD: Sounds like Borges, doesn't it? It's like Beethoven, his favorite piece of his own composition was Wellington's Victory, and he had to be forcibly restrained from conducting it on the platform.

(At this point Phil offered me my choice of one of two sandwiches, which he'd already purchased in anticipation of my visit.)

PKD: I bought a sandwich for you and a sandwich for me, and you get to choose which one you want. But your choice is limited to two. It's a binary question.

GR: Like your phrase, "Yes or no--choose one" which is in your work. I love that phrase.

PKD: My wife Annie used to say that.

GR: ...I wanted to ask you about "grate." Did you ever notice that? In just about all of your books, one character "grates" at another when he's angry.

PKD: I noticed that in your article, and I thought, he's referring to something I've used repeatedly as an idiom. But I'm not familiar with my own idiom.

GR: Well, I noticed it because I read all your books in a concentrated period. The word "grates" on me, and there it was in every book, at least once.

PKD: It's funny the way you start (noticing these things). You can't get away from it. It does come at you forever. Like, one time I was reading over one of my manuscripts, and the word "said" suddenly struck me as occurring far too many times. I know, theoretically, I'm trained to know that it's okay to say "said," and you should never try to say "expostulate ," "ejaculate," and all those other words for "said."(But) I noticed the word "said" 17 times on one page!

And from then on all I could see was the word "said," every page.

You just have to learn to live with it. I'm sorry about the word "grate." I'll never use it again. (laughing)

* * * * *

CHAPTER 7
"An Incredibly Conventional Writer"/ The Early Stories / The Form and The Craft / Markets of The Fifties / "Psionics" and John W. Campbell

4-22-81

PKD: You were very critical of my first period --
GR: I think too much so.
PKD: But it's true, but it's also remarkable, and I think you made that point, that somebody who was an incredibly conventional writer -- which is what I was in that first period --

My stories, for example, when I read them over, just appall me in that period. They're just appallingly bad stories. And not only are they bad, they're incredibly conventional. You wouldn't think the mind that conceived those conventional stories, would have made the quantum leaps up that I show later on. Without trying to be self-laudatory, the fact of the matter is that there **is** no indication in that early stuff that there's any unusual mind at work. The mind seems to be completely conventional. How I made those leaps, I don't know.

GR: (I tell Phil that even his earliest stories foreshadow all his future growth. I cite 1954's delicate fantasy "Upon the Dull Earth" and such chilling post-apocalypse tales as 1953's "Second Variety.")

PKD: Stylistically it's handled very well too. It's a very economical, non-pulp style.

My idea of a good story of mine, one that I really think is beautifully written, is one that inaugurates my last period, my most recent effusions --

GR: You might be on the verge of a whole new period.

PKD: Christ, I don't know.....is "A Little Something For Us Tempunauts" (1974). Which I think is very well written, very good. And I was influenced by John Sladek on that. Somebody had turned me on to Sladek. And I was just galvanized by the quality of his style. I suddenly realized --

In fact, that's one reason I got back into science fiction. I'd kind of given up there, after those disastrous years '71, '72. Just living off (the royalties). It really was moot, a question whether I'd ever write again. (Then) it wasn't moot. I really wanted to get back to writing.

10-12-81

GR: I wanted to ask you about the form and the craft of science fiction.

PKD: The craft comes in getting a lot of money. The form comes in the form of the outline you write to get to a lot of money. And the sample chapters that you write, that you find you can't do any more of because they don't go anywhere. So you leave it lay around for a couple of years and then they finally inquire, and then you sell them a book of used short stories instead, and they give you the same money for that. (laughs)

(Pauses, then seriously) The form and the craft of science fiction. Okay, I started off as a fantasy writer. I didn't start off as a science fiction writer. I wrote short fantasies for **F&SF (The Magazine of Fantasy and Science Fiction)**. And I only wrote science fiction because there was much more of a market (for it). And my early science fiction was **very bad.** I was a very **bad** science fiction writer, but I was a very good fantasy writer, but outside of Tony Boucher (editor of **F&SF**) nobody existed to buy fantasy.

And I wrote -- as Tom Disch has pointed out -- the most conventional science fiction imaginable. It all starts out with looking through the vid screen. "Captain! Look through the vid screen! I believe I see a strange object!" It's just execrable science fiction.

But the market continued to get better for science fiction and worse for fantasy. That gave me two choices. One, writing an awful lot of bad science fiction - 'cause I was getting a cent a word from **Planet Stories** - or writing better science fiction. And I chose the former. I wrote a lot of bad science fiction. Finally my agent said, I wish you would write fewer but better stories. Now, when your agent tells you that -- you're in trouble.

Somewhere the transition occurs, and I was able to write decent science fiction. And probably the transition occurs with **Eye on the Sky** (1957), which in a way is a fantasy.
GR: You found a way to incorporate fantasy into s.f.
PKD: Yeah. Because what must be taken into account is the state of the art in the early 50s. **Astounding** still dominated the field, with hard-core, nuts and bolts science fiction, the

Hal Clements stuff. The kind of science fiction that I do, that I do well, was not publishable then.

* * * * *

You see, the field was very limited at that time, as far as marketing. Ace Books was the only publisher of (science fiction) novels, I mean they really were, and the definition of science fiction in those days, in the mid-50s, was just incredibly limited. There was all this "psi" stuff that John W. Campbell (editor of **Astounding**) was promoting, and it had gotten to the point where he said psionics (telepathy, telekinesis, precognition, and other ESP powers) was the necessary premise for science fiction stories. Which is an incredible concept, that every science fiction story must have to do with psionics. No one had ever suggested before, ever, in the history of science fiction, that there was one topic and one topic only. Whether it's space travel, time travel, or the end of civilization.

He wrote me that psionics was a necessary premise in a science fiction story. Now that is really narrowing the field down. And Horace Gold, at **Galaxy,** only wanted sociological science fiction. That was all he would publish. So you had your choice. Now Campbell said you not only have to write about psionics, but the "psis" (the gifted) have to be in charge and they have to be good. They can neither be marginal nor can they be negative. And I wrote stories, and I had psis in (them), but the psis were either marginal or negative. (Such stories as "The Golden Man" and "A World of Talent," both 1954, feature conflict between the Normals and the superior Psis, who include such unappetizing specimens as the doughy, obese "Big Noodle" in "A World of Talent," gifted with "infinite parakinetic power and the mind of a moronic three-year-old." It was first published in **Galaxy**).

So they had to be three things, psis, and they had to be in

power, and they had to be good. Well, I'm telling you, that is incredible...Our idea of what was possible in science fiction was so barren of variety, that was finally happened was in 1959 science fiction almost ceased to exist.

Virtually every magazine folded. Most of the writers left the field. The pay rate went down to a half-cent a word, which is what it had been during the Depression. For all intents and purposes (with inflation), it was less.

I was looking through the magazines at that time, and I discovered there was only one new idea (that) had come into existence since H.G. Wells. And that was the idea of the corporate mind, where a number of entities form one mind, they form a group mind. And that was developed in a story by Nat Schachner in the 30s, in **Astounding.** So that preceded the war. So since World War II there wasn't a single new idea.

Because that whole psionics thing had been done by Olaf Stapleton in **Odd John** (1935), and (A.E. van Vogt's) **Slan** (1940) was a complete steal from **Odd John.** I have no idea if van Vogt knew that or not, that he had taken the entire idea of **Slan**, it's all in **Odd John.** (Both novels are about persecuted superhumans). The whole ambience, the role of the superior mutant, you know, who is hated and feared by all mankind.

Of course, that's what Campbell was trying to overcome, was that prejudice against psionics, that acute reaction against that.

* * * * *

CHAPTER 8
Donald Wollheim
Alternate Titles
Hard Science Fiction

10-12-81

GR: Let's talk about Don Wollheim.
PKD: Oh yeah, ol' Don Wollheim. He saved science fiction when it was dying. He was the only one going in those terrible years of the '50s. If he hadn't been publishing those Ace Doubles I think the field would have ended. It might have been resurrected in the '60s but I think there would

have been a total hiatus there. But he kept on. He never gave up publishing science fiction. Around '59, when it was so bad, he was after me to send him manuscripts. He was soliciting manuscripts. He was so strong and so courageous that he weathered that out. When the magazines all folded he weathered it out. The man has boundless courage and integrity. He has what I would regard as a rather conservative view of science fiction but the man is just all guts.

GR: You dedicated a book to him, I noticed.

PKD: And I meant it too. I have nothing to gain, I'm not expecting more of Don. I said that out of real feeling for him. The man has endured all these decades and has done so much for this field. He did not abandon science fiction during those terrible days in the late '50s. And everyone else did. The writers were giving up, the agents were giving up, the publishers were giving up, he stayed in business. He never gave up.

GR: What exactly was his position with Ace Books?

PKD: He was their Science Fiction editor. He had someone over him who was A.A. Wyn.

GR: How did you get along with him personally?

PKD: Very badly. He wrote very abusive letters, but they were honest letters. They weren't abusive for the sake of being abusive. He would just say, I think this is a terrible book, or a terrible story, or I think you're going in a terrible direction.

One thing he said, after reading a mainstream manuscript of mine, he said you will never make it as a mainstream writer. You simply do not have sufficient talent. He almost was right, in fact he may be right. He says as a science fiction writer you are an exceptional talent. As a mainstream writer you are just another failure.

That hurt. 'Cause I was really trying to sell those mainstream novels. But he said what he believed. But he did say as a science fiction writer you are an exceptional

talent. This is very early on, in the early '50s. You'll be a success in the field, you have what it takes. As far as the mainstream stuff goes you have nothing.
GR: Was **Solar Lottery** (his first published novel, by Ace in 1955) your first contact with him?
PKD: The first science fiction magazine I read was a Donald Wollheim magazine, **Stirring Science Stories.** But I had no contact with him until my agent sent **Solar Lottery** to him. And then he sent it back for **major** revisions.
GR: You followed his advice?
PKD: (laughs) Listen, he was the only market. That was it.
GR: How did he change it?
PKD: Oh, I don't remember now. Except it had to be exactly 6,000 lines long. But that was a marketing thing and I understood that. Ace Doubles were very, very precise as to how long those books were. But he did want a lot of changes made in that book, and a lot in **The World Jones Made** (1956), and we had a lot of fights about that. He wanted that to be much more commercial. I put in some of what I call literary elements.
GR: Like characterization.
PKD: Characterization! All the good things. He couldn't see any point in that. As far as **The Man Who Japed** (1957) goes, as Don says, it's the weakest of them all. I guess it's a question of which is the weakest, not which is the best.

But he did like **Eye in the Sky,** and he did bring it out as a single because he liked it, but he didn't tell me that. I learned that he had liked it because I read an ad that he had written. And he retitled most of them. **Solar Lottery, World Jones Made. The Man Who Japed** was my title. **Eye in the Sky** was his title.

(A partial list of Phil's original or working titles)

The World Jones Made................... "Womb for Another"
The Cosmic Puppets .... "A Glass of Darkness"

Eye in the Sky	"With Opened Mind"
The Simulacra	"First Lady of Earth"
Counter-Clock World	"The Dead Grow Young"
The Ganymede Takeover	"The Earth's Diurnal Course"
Ubik	"Death of an Anti-Watcher"
Deus Irae	"The Kneeling Legless Man"
The Divine Invasion	"Valis Regained"

* * * * *

(Returning to the topic of the idea drought of the late 50's):
PKD: There we were sitting around in 1959, and nobody had any ideas at all. And I wrote **Time Out of Joint** in '58, and we only got $750 for it. And we couldn't sell it as science fiction at all, we sold it to Lippincott as a "novel of menace." And Donald Wollheim read that - it got submitted to Ace by mistake - and Wollheim --

I've never read such a long, angry letter from an editor in my life. He was incredibly threatened by that novel. He saw everything that he construed as science fiction as going down the tubes with what that novel did. If it ever got into print, which he doubted it ever would, he said the only thing salvageable was the last chapter, where there was the war on the moon. And I should build back from the last chapter. And the style was wrong, because it was essentially pedestrian, he said...

But we were stuck with the Sam Moskowitz-Donald Wollheim idea of what constituted science fiction in those days. And I've always said the epitome of it was Hal Clement's **Mission of Gravity** (1953). It's incredible. I was reading a synopsis -- it came out as a serial in **Astounding.** I picked up the second issue, 'cause it had my story. I looked at the synopsis and it says, for the first time in human history it was possible to measure three gravitational fields at once.

What kind of premise is that for a novel? In 1972, I was at the Wellscon in L.A. And I got up on the stand - I was called on unexpectedly to speak, I thought it was just going to be a round table discussion - and I got up and started talking about science fiction. I mentioned **Mission of Gravity.** I said, I conceived of a sequel, where somebody for the first time invents a tape measure that will roll up, instead of walking around with a yard stick. So the synopsis would read, "For the first time in human history it was possible to carry a yardstick rolled up in the form of a tape measure in your pocket, and then you could measure everything that you came across." (laughing) You would meet your girl friend and you would measure her and she'd be five feet four, so after that you'd refer to her as "Five Feet Four."And a tree would be "Twelve Feet Nine."

And that was the kind of ideas we were stuck with in 1959. And everybody was leaving the field. I left the field and went into the jewelry business, working with my wife (Anne).

* * * * *

CHAPTER 9
The Sixties / Ellison and Wollheim / Origin of Dr. Bloodmoney / Dangerous Visions / Hate Mail / Counterfeits

10-12-81

PKD: The kind of stuff that I do now, there was no market for that at all. Nobody would publish it. And for one thing, it didn't exist, the kind of stuff I do now.
GR: Did you create that market?
PKD: No, no, no . Harlan Ellison created that market with

Dangerous Visions (his 1967 anthology of original stories).
GR: But that was what, '66, '67. Your (outrageous) stuff was '64.
PKD: Right, I lied. Harlan didn't create that market. I said that to make Harlan like me 'cause he hates me so.

Actually the big turning point for me then was **The Man in the High Castle** (1962).
GR: But that was for you. What about the field?
PKD: There was no field at that time.
GR: The field was zip circa 1959.
PKD: Right. There was no use writing for a field that didn't exist. What I did was simply write as good a book as I could when I wrote **The Man in the High Castle.** And it was not purchased as science fiction, it was not advertised as science fiction. It was picked up by the Science Fiction Book Club, and that's why it got the Hugo Award. If they hadn't picked it up it wouldn't have won.

I saw the ad that Putnam ran in **The New York Times.** In no way was it presented as science fiction.
GR: But there was a boom in the field in the '60s.
PKD: Yes. And a lot of that was due to Harlan. He gets the credit. And there were a lot of new writers coming in that were real good. That was the other side. Harlan couldn't get real good stories out of a turnip. There had to be the writers to do it. There were good people coming in, people like (Roger) Zelazny, Chip Delany, all the guys.
GR: Tell me about Harlan Ellison.
PKD: He's probably done more for science fiction than any other person in the field except Don Wollheim. And they were working at complete cross purposes. Don Wollheim's working for conventional science fiction, Harlan's working for experimental science fiction. And between the two of them they've done a lot to protect, preserve, and encourage the field.

Because you could go one way or the other. You could go

toward Wolheim or you could go towards Ellison. Ellison in the **Dangerous Visions** series proved himself to be the greatest editor that ever entered the field. He didn't just take stories that had been written, but he went to you and demanded that you do your best.

Now that was not the first time that was tried. The first time was for something called "Project C." They had a lot of money. Bill Kemp was one of the people involved in that. They contacted me, and they told me, we want you to write the most experimental science fiction story you can write, for this anthology. Virtually what Harlan asked for.

Well, I wrote them a story, which I don't even have now, which they bought, and paid a lot of money for and gave me an extra $50 bonus for because they said it was so good. And then they found - and I'm not saying this to make myself look good - they said they're cancelling the project because they cannot find enough stories to make a collection of. They said your story was exactly what we were looking for. We couldn't get enough to make up the anthology and we have abandoned it; you can keep the money. It was quite a bit of money. I didn't even keep a copy of the story. And do you know what the story turned out to be? It was the basis for **Dr. Bloodmoney.** It was about Hoppy Harrington on his cart. It was a novelette version of **Dr. Bloodmoney** if you can imagine that. Everything that was in the story went into the book so there's nothing lost.

So Harlan was not the first, he was the first **successful** one. Harlan **was** able to generate the response. And one of the ways he did that was the letter that he wrote us. He was so forceful and so convincing that he brought us out of our torpor, all of us. For me it was like rolling off a log, 'cause I wanted to do that kind of stuff, it was what I wanted to do. I mean it was just like, exactly the kind of invitation I craved and hoped for. More conventional writers found it difficult

I believe. My impression in reading some of their writing in **Dangerous Visions** (was) that it was somewhat **embarassing** to write a controversial story. They did not enjoy writing controversial stuff. I love it. I thrive on controversy. I mean, I have a bad attitude, as I've said many times. I would like to write an offensive story that offends everybody. Like my anti-abortion story ("The Pre-Persons," 1974). It didn't bother me a bit that it offended a lot of people. That didn't have any effect on me, to get hate mail. All I do is just recycle it into the comments I make later. I say I got a lot of hate mail, it gives me ammunition. It's no use sending me hate mail.

GR: Do you get a lot of hate mail? Love mail?

PKD: I get some of each. I get mostly good stuff. But I get some pretty, pretty vicious letters from time to time. And no wonder, look what I wrote about drugs, communism, anti-abortion stuff, God. If there's an area where people are in dispute I'll find it and seek it out.

GR: But that's now. What kind of mail did you get in the '50s?

PKD: I didn't get anything. I got no mail. I got one letter on **Eye in the Sky** from a guy whose book I had read. Murray Teigh Bloom was his name. He'd written a book on numismatics, on counterfeiting coins, that I had read and he read **Eye in the Sky** and said it would make a wonderful movie. It was the first fan letter I ever got. It just so happened I had just read Mr. Bloom's book and was able to write back and say I had read your book on numismatics and it was an excellent book.

As a matter of fact it was that book (which I have identified as **Money of Their Own: the Great Counterfeiters,** 1957) that gave me the idea about forgeries. He said a really good counterfeit coin can never be nicked. So there may be classes of counterfeiting that no one ever (catches). (laughs)

So that's where I got the idea of what the Greeks called **dokein** ("to seem"), which is like the Veil of Maya, but originally meant a coin counterfeited so well that even when the authorities detected it they continued to let it circulate.

They called it a **dokein,** like you find in the Christian heresy Docetism. Docetics believed that Christ's body was not really there, that there was no physical body, there only seemed to be a body. It was such a good imitation no one could tell the difference. It ate food, but it walked through walls, as you find in the Gospels. Jesus entered where they were eating through a closed door. Well, that's where the Doscetics get their idea. That's the Gnostics, the Christian term for Gnostics.

* * * * *

CHAPTER 10
Harlan Ellison
Reader Response
Publishers and Agents
Deus Irae Censored

10-12-81

GR: How do you and Harlan Ellison get along?
PKD: Well, I've known Harlan since '54 and he was this twirp fan then, and he asked me for a story for his twirp fanzine. And I gave him an unpublished story and he never published it, 'cause it wasn't good enough. (laughs) That's how we started out.

He was this typical pushy twirp fan, with this grating voice that could be heard throughout the entire convention. It's just as obnoxious as hell, you know. And later on he started writing stories and I said to Tony Boucher one day, "It seems like all the stories now are being written by Bob Silverberg and Harlan Ellison." And he said yes, and one of them is good and one is terrible. And I said "Which is good?" and he said Bob Silverberg.

I don't like Harlan's writing. There are a couple of things he's done that I think are masterpieces. It's really strange, 'cause when Harlan is good, he is so good that he's better than everyone else.

Now Harlan can't fathom my attitude. He thinks -- it's like Joanna (Russ) when she thinks I am saying two things at once. But I have read things by Harlan that were masterpieces. But the bulk of the corpus, the total opus, is as far as I'm concerned worthless, with exceptions of tremendous stature.

GR: Which ones did you like?

PKD: I don't remember, "A Boy and His Dog" or something like that. The one where he buries the dog. The dog dies. (As the dog is far from being dead and buried in "A Boy and His Dog", it is possible Phil was thinking of something else, less gruesome than that story by Ellison). I said that in public, at a lecture I was giving at Cal State Fullerton. I said that story would be read for as long as the English language is spoken. And I meant it. I mean it now.

* * * * *

Now, I've had people tell me, sit right on the couch where you're sitting right now and say, I've tried to read your writing and I find it unreasonable. "Unreasonable!" Unreadable. (laughs) All those things. And I say, that's okay, we can still be friends as people. For all I know, you're an artist and I don't like your painting. But let's leave it out of the conversation though. Let's agree that if you don't like my writing, at least let's not talk about it. Don't sit here and tell me why my writing is no good.

This one guy came by with his girlfriend and she said (whiney voice)"Michael lent me one of your books and I couldn't get through it and I thought it was awful." And I liked her a real lot. And I said, please Katy. She was smart enough not to push the point. I thought she was really great.

Now Harlan can't do that. If somebody doesn't like his writing, to Harlan that person is a monster. I know lots of people that I really like, who don't like my writing. I know lots of people that I really like who don't **read** my writing and never heard of me. When I was in the drug sub-culture none of them had heard of me. They never read anything. I was perfectly happy. I don't give a shit.

Nobody is universally liked. Henry Miller once said Shakespeare was the greatest bore in the English language. And I'm sure if he had ever met Shakespeare he would have told him so.

I don't like people to be abusive about it. One woman, I lent her a book of short stories. She started one and simply threw the book across the room she was so repelled by it. When it gets to that point, the author has a right --

Well, down at the savings and loan I gave a copy of **VALIS** to the chick in charge, and she said I tried to read it, but frankly I can't get through those morbid, self-indulgent things where everybody's sick and crying and killing themselves and crazy. She says I read for enjoyment. And I said "You have a brain, Madame, the size of a BB." But we're still good friends. I put up with what she says and she puts up with what I say. And she's real cute 'cause she walks up to me and she says "You have all this money and you're still wearing those awful old clothes? What in the world is the matter with you?" And I say I'll take my account to Home Savings. Give me a pen. And she says no I won't.

I don't have a lot of ego tied into my writing. In fact I don't really care exactly -- in meeting somebody. People always use the same expression: "He's your greatest fan." Well what do I care? What difference does that make to me? That's his problem. That's his business, not my business. We do not have a contractual relationship. I'll tell you one time this really got to me. This one girl I was really fond of -- in fact she was my girlfriend in Canada -- said "Your letters are depressing, your books are depressing, and you're depressing." So I got out a dollar - she had a copy of some book of mine - what's the one Ursula liked so much? - **Ganymede,** no, **Galactic Pot Healer.** She found it depressing. I got out a dollar and said "I'll buy it back from you." And her response to that was "No, I'll read anything." That did irritate me.

She'd included me and my letters to her -- I'd written her these real soulful letters saying I can't live without you. And she found that depressing. Pouring my heart out to this dizzy broad.

I don't judge people on whether they like my writing. In that case I'd be this one great ego floating against the ceiling like a helium balloon. And therefore I'd be vulnerable to everything that everybody said. If they said something good the balloon would float higher, if they said something bad the balloon would float lower.

GR: Weren't you that way when you started off?
PKD: No, never have been.
GR: How about the stuff you were really proud of -- I know you were depressed when you couldn't get **Martian Time-Slip** (1965) published. (See Chapter 22)
PKD: Well that was a marketing thing. That was not a reader response. The reader response has always been good on **Martian Time-Slip**. That's another issue.
GR: You make a distinction then between marketing people, publishing people, and --

PKD: Oh yes. If you can't sell your book, that's really terrible. There's no way you can laugh that off. You can laugh off somebody saying I tried to read your writing and couldn't read it, because you know other people are reading it. But if no publisher will publish it, then you've written it in vain. And I don't care if the publisher likes it. I just care if he publishes it. He may say I'm buying it because it has commercial value. Name value. In fact, even if the publisher says I thought it was marvelous, I don't even care for an analysis of why it was marvelous. It's my agent (Russell Galen) whose response I treasure as far as the marketability and the literary thing as a unified thing. For he's able somehow to judge them simultaneously. He's an agent, which means he's got to sell it, but he's also a literate man, which means he's got to judge it. So he operates on two axes simultaneously. If everybody was like him, books would be sold according to their literary value. If you clone him and put him charge of the whole field, all the problems would disappear because the one criterion would be literary excellence.

However you then have the problem of achieving that excellence, because he is very demanding. When he first started reading the Angel Archer book, he called me up and said I can't read this. And that shut me down. There's no hope for this at all.

He's never really repudiated that view. He said I did finish it, I did turn it over to Simon and Schuster and it was okay. But he never raved about it. I mean I was convinced it had failed. I could see Simon and Schuster saying, "A 21 year old woman? That's got to go. Rewrite the book from the standpoint of a head of lettuce. Angel Archer has to go." They didn't ask for any revisions.

That's the thing you always fear. The very thing you wrote the book for, the purpose of writing the book, is the thing they won't want. That happened to me one time, in an outline for Doubleday. The thing that I wrote the outline for - the one thing that was my **raison d'etre** for the book - they wanted it removed. That was with **Deus Irae,** where he painted with his tongue (quadraplegic Tibor McMastors was to paint with only his tongue). That's why I couldn't write the book (eventually completed by Roger Zelazny). There are actually quadraplegics who do paint with their tongues, and he (Tibor) had servo-assists, so it was relatively easy.

* * * * *

CHAPTER 11
Academic Critics
Scanner and Teilhard
Darko Suvin

4-22-81

(I had been praising the critically neglected **Counter-Clock World** to Phil).
PKD: You see, that's one of the reasons I was so impressed by your analysis. In no way were you prejudiced in **your** appraisal of a book by the conventional (ideas held toward) the book by prior critics. In other words, you approached

each book based on your own appraisal, not on a formula that had been devised by (others).

(At this point Phil heaps praise on my writing, and of course this is the one place the tape broke - kippled - in the machine, first time I listened to it. Oh well, I have my memories).

GR: I don't know what to say.

PKD: That's true, and I'll illustrate it for you. I could show you examples. (fishes out a scholarly journal) This is an example of the incredibly stupid, pernicious, affected, pompous, meaningless academic crap that gets written. This character studied **Scanner** (**A Scanner Darkly**), and all he does is wind up talking about Teilhard de Chardin. Because I quote from Teilhard in the goddamned book. Luckman reads a few sentences. So this guy leaps to the conclusion that the secret to **Scanner** lies in Teilhard de Chardin. And then goes on to analyze Teilhard de Chardin.

The reason Luckman quotes from that book is that it happened to be the book closest at hand to me when I was writing that page. It's of no importance what Luckman reads at that moment. It's just that he reads something that is not related to what's going on, that has no relevance to what's happening. So he's completely detatched from what's going on.

So picking a book at random was the way to do that, to completely detach the content of the book from the narrative. Now this guy assumes that's the key to the goddamned novel. (The episode in question is in Chapter Eight of **Scanner.** I was going to try and defend the poor academic's intitiative - who else but Phil would have Teilhard de Chardin on Christ's reality close at hand when writing a novel about drugs? And it is Phil's sensibility that informs the whole work. But Phil is right, the quote has no relationship to the scene at hand other than what he says it has, as a marker of Luckman's disassociation from his fellows).

These people are crazy. They're simply nuts.

* * * * *

(I told Phil what had inspired me to write my piece on him was frustration at finding the critics I read dismissing his post-'65 work as minor, and that they centered on the same few novels all the time as his only important work: **Man in the High Castle, Three Stigmata of Palmer Eldritch,** sometimes **Dr. Bloodmoney** or **Ubik**).

PKD: What the critics and especially the academic critics have done (is to dismiss my later work), and they don't have to deal with an ongoing process. That makes their work for them much easier. But this is very destructive to the author involved, for the author very soon gets the impression that he has done his good, his best writing already, and he did it some time ago. He did it fifteen, twenty years ago. This has a very pernicious effect on the author's drive to go on working.

GR: Has that depressed you?

PKD: No, 'cause I don't pay any attention.

But if you did pay attention to it -- I mean, Darko Suvin just flat out says he hasn't gotten anything out of anything I've written since **Man in the High Castle.** He thinks that I peaked about 1963. It isn't even a bell-shaped curve, you know. I just fell right off the chart.

I think it's the worse news a writer can get, that he did his best work fifteen years ago, and is obviously never going to do anything good again as long as he lives.

(Suvin's essay, "Artifice as Refuge and World View: Philip K. Dick's Foci," appeared in **Science-Fiction Studies** in 1975, and was reprinted in the Olander-Greenberg anthology **Philip K. Dick** in 1983. Phil's characterization of it is essentially correct: "I believe," Suvin intones, "Dick's major works, from **The Man in the High Castle** to **Dr.**

Bloodmoney, have been written." And this in 1975! Suvin does qualify this somewhat by hoping that Dick, "in the middle of his life's path," will prove him wrong by again "chang(ing)...startlingly." (Suvin, as an academic leftist, is upset that Dick abandoned the political concerns of his early '60s books in favor of the "solitary anxieties" of "unexplainable ontological puzzles" in his novels after 1966. In this Suvin pre-echoes Ursula LeGuin's expressed concern that Dick was "trying to sovle probably unresolvable metaphysical problems."

(Phil, as quoted above and in this book's chapter on LeGuin, more than adequately responds to his "eminently sane" critics. I would go further to say that unlike Suvin with his search for "significant humanistic literature" and LeGuin with her wholesome parables, Dick achieved greatness by plunging into the depths of his, and mine, and your, "solitary anxieties." There is, after all, more to the universe than being politically correct and adopting healthy sex roles).

* * * * *

CHAPTER 12
Multiple Viewpoints / Will Cook / Exploring All Possible Viewpoints James Joyce Third Person Female

4-22-81

(Phil explained how his favored "multi-focus viewpoint" did not appear in his early science fiction, or in his early literary novels).

PKD: You've got to realize that they (most of his literary novels) were written before **Time Out of Joint,** they were written before that. They came around the time that I wrote

The World Jones Made (and dating back to his first plunge into writing, in 1951).

They're really very early novels, and I had no control over viewpoint then. I only got control over viewpoint because of a chance remark, a friend of mine, a Western writer named Will Cook -- who's now dead, who dropped dead from overwork at the age of 46, which made a profound impression on me (laughs). Shit! Is this the rewards of creative endeavors, to drop dead at the age of 46? -- I was then in my 20s, you know. I thought, when I get to be around 46, I'm going to slow down enormously.

But he found out that I varied my viewpoint, and I didn't even know of the concept "viewpoint." I was so naive and so amateurish. So I asked him what my viewpoint was, he says, sometimes it's third person omniscient, sometimes it's third person interior, something like that. It's like suddenly being equipped for the first time with such concepts as ontology. And I said, "Gollee!" I just fathomed what he was saying. So I said, well, are there any other kinds of viewpoints? He said, Oh, yeah! there's first person, you know, and he explained to me all about viewpoint.

And I just memorized everything he said. I thought, "Goddamn! This is really great! I can do all kinds of things I didn't know." In **Solar Lottery,** there's a scene in the first chapter, where I could not fathom how to handle the viewpoint. I literally did not know about interior third person versus omniscience. So I was having a hell of a time. So he clued me in to all that stuff.

So once I got into the viewpoint problem as a problem, I decided to explore all the possible viewpoints that might exist, not just the ones that were conventionally used. Like he said, there's just three viewpoints, really. There's third person omniscient, there's first person -- there's actually first person real interior, like James Joyce did in **Ulysses.** I knew that. Like you're almost getting down in the unconscious. -- And then there's third person interior, versus third person external. And he explained the difference to me.

I said, Well, shit! I'll bet I can think of another viewpoint (laughs). Like having a whole lot of people walking around with interior viewpoints, you know. That's where I developed the multi-foci third person interior, was I tried all the logical possibilities. It was almost random.

I was just entranced by this viewpoint. I said, the key to writing, the key to fiction writing, is viewpoint. 'Cause I had read **Ulysses,** and really loved it, and really studied it, and really studied it very carefully. And it made a big impression on me. I realized, that's the thing that makes **Ulysses** great is the viewpoint. Joyce had found a new viewpoint to write from, that no one had ever found before. It's much deeper in the psyche than anybody else's. I'm sure everyone knows this. But to me it was a great revelation. Like the last part, the last chapter of **Ulysses,** with Molly Bloom's stream of consciousness.

And then I had really studied **Finnegan's Wake,** and I had noticed that **Finnegan's Wake** ends - I've never seen this pointed out anywhere - with a third person interior female viewpoint, deep within the psyche of a woman. And much more beautiful than **Ulysses.** As beautiful as the ending of **Ulysses** is, the ending of **Finnegan's Wake** is even more beautiful.

So I go, this is the **ultimate** viewpoint; third person female very interior. Which is what I'm trying to do in this goddamn novel **(Timothy Archer)** that I'm working on now. It's sensitive, it's tender, it's comprehensive, you know what I mean? It's idiomatic. It allows the greatest latitude in terms of the character development. It permits the greatest development of character imaginable. That's the advantage of that point of view. It's not valuable in terms of an overview of the actions of the plot. That's where the omniscient viewpoint is useful. But the third person interior tunes you into the thoughts of the person beautifully. That to me is ideal.

I always wondered what Joyce would have written had he lived longer? What **possibly** could have followed **Finnegan's Wake?** Could you imagine what he would have been faced with to surmount that, in terms of evolution of your books, from **Dubliners** to **Portrait of an Artist,** to **Ulysses.** So he's sitting there, he's written **Finnegan's Wake** -- What now? What the hell am I going to do now? (chuckles) Go back to the sparse prose style like **Dubliners.** Write two columns parallel on the page like (Samuel) Delany did in **Dhalgren** (1975).

I guess it's a good thing he died after writing **Finnegan's Wake,** because there's no way -- !

GR: It satisfied the academics. Now, a female viewpoint is better than male, in terms of sensitivity?

PKD: Yeah, well because of the practice against men being sensitive emotionally. It's a way of overcoming the image that men have to maintain. In other words, this is a form of chauvinism. It's an anti-masculine chauvinism, it's not an anti-feminist thing; that men do not have sensitive feelings, that men are "tough" and "strong." Like if you have a man thinking those thoughts, he's a wimp. So it don't work.

* * * * *

CHAPTER 13
Themes and Motifs: Hard Science
Counter-Clock World
Galactic Pot-Healer
Aliens / Desmesnes
Neanderthals
Policemen

4-22-81

GR: Do you do much scientific research for your books? I was reading **Martian Time Slip** the other day, and you had this party of Bleekman dying for lack of water, and this satellite registering their location "at gyrocompass point 4.65003" on Mars. Did you look this up on a Martian globe, or check this with your scientific friends -- ?

PKD: No. I made it up.

GR: Do you research things? I'm not much into hard science at all, which is probably why I don't like hard science fiction, but I was reading the other day that there were three types of gravity --

PKD: Small, medium, and large. (laughter)

GR: But I read somebody somewhere that said your science was generally accurate.

PKD: My science is accurate? Christ, I don't even know how many planets there are.

GR: Because they (hard science fans) will complain bitterly about **Counter-Clock World.** You ask them to believe "six impossible things in the first chapter." (Most of the carping about this novel, to which Phil responds here, is in Bruce Gillespie's anthology **Philip K. Dick: Electric Shepherd).**

PKD: Fine, let's see them write a book with time moving backward. Start with the final punctuation and devolve back to the opening world.

GR: But I love **Counter-Clock World!**

PKD: There is no way that you can have people with time moving backward and write a coherent book unless you have people violate their premises. Some things still have to procede forward in linear time. Thank you, I'm glad you liked it.

I liked the little opening script, the opening chapter quotes from Erigena and Aquinas. I spent more time gathering those little quotes together -- they're not just random, they're not easy quotes to find. They're pretty damned embedded in the corpus of Christian mystical thought. They're just very good, I was noticing that the other day. You can almost reconstruct medieval mysticism out of Erigena's quotes.

* * * * *

(We were talking of his writing himself into a corner on his latest novel).

GR: Is this how you wrote your other novels? Some of them seem like they were made up as you went along, in great spurts of invention.

PKD: That's correct, especially with **Galactic Pot-Healer.**

GR: Oh, really? That's a great favorite of mine. Just sort of improvised?

PKD: Oh, completely. Ol' Brunner, John Brunner said to me one time about **Galactic Pot Healer,** that got away from you completely, didn't it? And I said, yeah, it completely got away from me.

But it didn't get away from me in the sense that it was running ahead of me, that I was trying to catch up with it. I mean, I was the one who was dragging it along behind me. I was winging it, but I was the one who was doing the work. That novel did not write itself. That was a very difficult novel to write. Because once I established that kind of soaring quality, you know, where they just move so rapidly, it was very hard to maintain. I was afraid I would fall back into that opening sort of dreary monotonous thing that he's stuck with (the book's hero on Earth), and lose the whole point of the book that way.

So once I took off, I had to keep it going. In a way the book got away from me, but in a way I had to carry the book all the way to the end.

I liked that book. You know, you made some interesting points (in your essay), like sometimes books, like the Books of the Kalends (in **Galactic Pot Healer**) tell the truth, and sometimes they lie. Which is a very interesting point. And sometimes aliens -- what'd you say?

GR: Sometimes they can be trusted, like Morgo Rahn Wilc in **Frolix 8,** and sometimes they cannot be trusted, like the vugs in **Game Players of Titan.** The whole question in **Frolix 8** is, can this alien be trusted? The one the astronaut is returning inside of, and Morgo is trying to reassure him of his goodness.

PKD: I would essentially try to view aliens as benign, just in reaction to the sort of thing (Robert) Heinlein did in **The Puppet Masters** (1953), where you mistrust the alien merely on the basis that it's an alien.

GR: That goes back to **The World Jones Made,** where everyone gangs up to destroy the innocent "drifters" (helpless alien blobs that land on earth) and as a result the Earth is isolated,quarantined.

PKD: I was amazed. I read **The World Jones Made** recently. I hadn't read it in years, and I realized something that I had completely forgotten. I wrote that at a time when I was still writing mainstream experimental novels. And that shows up in **The World Jones Made,** the attempt to do something other than "mere science fiction," as I regarded it at the time.

9-30-81

GR: The notion of feudal desmesnes, vast tracts of land controlled by one person, recurs a lot in your books **(The Game Players of Titan, The Penultimate Truth).**

PKD: That was - when the Roman Empire broke up - Rome had actually become somewhat decentralized. Italy had fallen into obscurity, and the wealth had all passed to Gaul, France. And there were these huge, huge estates called desmesnes, where the wealthy Roman citizens would go and live, and these formed the basis for the feudal barons, castles, in the Middle Ages. When Rome fell the desmesnes in France continued on, and they became the basis for England and France (eventually).

GR: So why do you have them in your books?

PKD: Because they're symbols for capital. The feudal barons -- their vast holdings. Holdings expressed in terms of land. The American South was that way, those plantations were like desmesnes (without) the fortified castles.

* * * * *

GR: You like to use aboriginals, "primitive" type peoples in several of your works (**The Simulacra, Martian Time-Slip,** etc).
PKD: Yeah, and that's in that unpublished one, **The Man Whose Teeth Were All Exactly Alike.** (Neanderthals) had no incisors, they were all molars, 'cause he chewed seeds a lot, like sheep do.

I just have always felt very sorry for Neanderthal Man. I think he got a bad break. He was essentially a timid creature. He wasn't a hunter. He usually lived on fruits and nuts and berries and herbs and bugs, and animals killed by other animals. He was in no way a fresh predator, and he got aced out by Cro-Magnon man, who was an expert hunter...the tools that Neanderthal Man left us are so primitive compared to Cro-Magnon's tools.

I figured that Neanderthal with that mandible, with those teeth had a lot of trouble talking. It must have been very difficult for them to articulate just because of the mandible.

* * * * *

GR: Policemen recur as figures in many of your novels, usually rather sympathetically (**Flow My Tears, Do Androids Dream, The Divine Invasion**).
PKD: You see, I figure that if I write about cops as if they're real nice, then when I'm stopped on the freeway they're going to be real nice to me.
GR: So how many policemen have read your books?
PKD: Well they have to read the book, and they have to stop me, so that's a population of zero.

It's an ambivalence I have toward authority. I would really like to make friends with the police. I'm afraid if I start depicting cops the way I look at them, (A) it will appear that I'm paranoid - God knows that's true about cops, I am paranoid about cops - and (B) I will antagonize them just that much more. So I start to write about them because I am just obsessed by cops as images of the dehumanized creature. And then I start to humanize them, really out of motives of fear. I start to create a dangerous cop, and then I think this is scaring me, I'll make him real nice. He just looks dangerous. Underneath he's got a heart of gold.

I would like to come to a modus vivendi with the police. I would really like to bury the hatchet with the police. I just don't know if it's ever going to be possible for me. I'm head of a committee in this building (his apartment house), and I've got two cops on my committee, and the first night I walk in and saw two cops sitting there, I just about dropped dead. And they made me head of the committee too. And I was wearing my Haight Ashbury Free Clinic T-shirt, and everything.

* * * * *

CHAPTER 14
Fans and Fellow Writers
Disch and Spinrad
Michael Moorcock and "The Skull"
Robert Silverberg
"Life is Predicated on Human Love"
(comment by Robert Silverberg)

10-12-81

GR: How have you gotten along with the fans over the years? I gather there's a whole subculture of them I know very little about.

PKD: Well, I used to run with fans at conventions, but they were all into the conventions, and I'm not into conventions, so I don't tend to see many of them anymore.

Fans always notice misprints in your books, where you spell a word wrong or get a name wrong, and they memorize all these things and they come up to you and say "On page 34 of **Deus Irae** you have Hagia Sophia spelled with two g's, and it only has one g 'cause I looked it up. What do you say to that?" and I say "Well, if you're so smart, why don't you write the novels" -- no, I always say "You're right." I always agree when they find something in one of my books. "You said on page 12 that she had red hair and on page 98 you said she has black hair." I say "You're right. You're absolutely right." I just completely agree with any error, fault -- like one guy came up to me and said "In **Man in the High Castle** you left the second umlaut off Gotterdammerung." I says, "Have you no further words to say to me about that book, sir?" "No," he says, "that's it." I says thank you and goodbye.

* * * * *

GR: I wanted to ask you about your colleagues -- you're friends, I understand, with Tom Disch and Norman Spinrad.
PKD: I met Spinrad as a person before I read much of his work, and liked him as a person; I also liked his work. With Disch I started out reading his writing and contacted him to let him know how much I liked his writing. So the two are a reversal, mirror images.
  I forget when I met Spinrad. It was at a convention.
GR: You have a really funny short story, which you haven't had reprinted, set at a science fiction convention.
PKD: Yeah, yeah, "Waterspider" (1964). A lot of the conversation in there did occur, like the conversation between me and van Vogt; that literally transpired between us. It's really funny because after it came out, I got a letter from van Vogt and he said that I had figured out what he would have said, but actually he **had** said all that to me. But

he didn't remember because I was nobody to him then. It was '54 (when they conversed).

* * * * *

GR: Do you know Michael Moorcock?
PKD: I don't know anything about him. I know he's in this area here - he's in L.A. - and I have his phone number. Spinrad gave it to me. He's written some very nice things about me. I don't know his writing at all.
GR: Call him up some time, if he likes your stuff.
PKD: Well, I should, shouldn't I? But you see, then I'm in the position where I haven't read his stuff.

I read one story by him, about Jesus being a mongoloid idiot. ("Behold the Man," 1966. It appeared in the same issue of the British magazine **New Worlds,** No. 166, September 1966, that John Brunner's groundbreaking praise of Dick's novels appeared in, and was later expanded to novel form. It deals with an extremely unpleasant, neurotic scientist being transported back in time to ancient Palestine, in search of Jesus, and winds up with the character "becoming" Jesus and being crucified, without any gain of nobility in his character. It is considered a seminal "New Wave" taboo-breaking work -- Dick at that time being praised as a precursor of that 1960s rebellion).
GR: I hated that story.
PKD: I did too. It was too long, too. The point could have been made in about half the wordage. And it's a dumb idea. It's evident by the third word that the guy himself is going to turn out to be the Savior. And I wrote that once, in a story called "The Skull" (**If** magazine, September 1952, not reprinted), which is one of the first horror stories of mine ever published, the first one (of mine in) **If** magazine. It was about a guy sent back in time to kill the Savior (in this case, of an unspecified religion). And he's given the Savior's skull. And he goes back in time, and he's standing there getting ready to walk out into that world, in the costume of

that time period, and he's holding the skull, and he suddenly sees that it's his own skull. He realizes that **he** is the Savior. And he tries to get back into the future quick enough, but he is already back in the past when he discovers it, and somebody sees him and says "My God, you've been resurrected!" It's too late, they've seen him, as the resurrected Savior.

In a way, my story is even more subtle. Just by being back there - he missed the time, he got there after the guy had been killed - (he guarantees the religion he'd been sent to prevent).

* * * * *

GR: Do you know Robert Silverberg?
PKD: Oh, yeah, sure. I've known Silverberg for years. Silverberg always comes up to you and says your beard is cut wrong. That's the wrong style. Or he says that girl's too young for you. He assumes a worldly-wise, sophisticated stance, as if he knows everything, and the truth of the matter is that Bob is a very tender, loving and gentle person, a very sensitive person who's been hurt very badly. He told me that once. I don't know if I should talk about it, but he did tell me that he had suffered in that divorce from Barbara to the point where he found it unbearable and that he knew that I would understand because I had gone through many a divorce. He let down his guard just that one time. It was genuine, real. He said I know everyone thinks that I'm rich and successful, but I'm really hurting. I'm hurting real bad. I'm paraphrasing of course - he said, what the **fuck** good has it done me, to make all this money, and sell all these book and be all this, and then to have my marriage break up. I know you'll understand, and I sure did.

In the final analysis, life is predicated on human love, mutual human love, and when that goes you can write like Kafka and Joyce and Virginia Woolf put together and it don't feed the admiral's cat. You are just as damned and as doomed as if you had illustrated Snatch comics. I mean it's all the same when it comes down to this business of human relationships. Look -- I tied a knot in my Orange Crush can just thinking about it. (And he had, crushing while he spoke).

That's the terrible thing. One time I was sitting here, feeling real terrible. My girlfriend had just moved out. And I'm sitting here all by myself, in the apartment we had rented together. And I look across the room, to that glass door cabinet with all my books. And I said, "I brought you to life" -- and I was serious, 'cause I was a little fucked up. I said, "I brought you to life, every one of you I created, I gave you to the world. Now, can't you give me anything back?" And those books just sat there. Those books could not give me back anything.

I just felt -- I had given these books years, just decades of my life and now when I needed something my books were mute. They were not eloquent, they were mute.

Actually, that's not true. I probably could have gleaned some sort of surcease by going through some of the books. I expected the books to pop off the shelf and come over and console me, I suppose. I don't know. I just looked at them and felt, what an irony. Here's this whole goddamned cabinet full of books, here I am sitting with my girlfriend moved out.

I was thinking the other night, Goethe once said, the peasant with his wife and children and little cottage is happier than the greatest creative artist in the world who is writing in splendid isolation. And if Goethe said it, it's probably true, because Goethe was no fool.

I don't know why this is. It doesn't bring **me** any happiness. On the other hand, if I wasn't a writer I think I'd be more miserable. I think there's degrees of misery. But the final thing that makes it worthwhile are the people in your life. And in that regard you differ from no one else.

You are in the same boat with everyone else. You live by your relationships, you live by your friends and loved ones.

(Robert Silverberg kindly gave me an okay to print all of Phil's comments on his private life. He wrote me on February 4, 1984, "the situation that was causing me such distress at the time (1977) was a separation, not a divorce. The divorce still hasn't happened after all these years, though the separation continues (a lot more amicably than it looked when I was discussing it with Phil.")

* * * * *

CHAPTER 15

Ursula K. LeGuin "Going Crazy in Santa Ana"/ "Unresolvable Metaphysical Problems" "Hateful Women" / The Lathe of Heaven and Ubik / Phil's Sensitivity (Letter from Ursula K. LeGuin) / Feminism and "The Pre-Persons"

4-22-81

(We had been talking about Phil's adoption of a female viewpoint in his Timothy Archer project, and the scope that viewpoint gives to sensitivity).

PKD: This is really very interesting, because Ursula (LeGuin) has been accusing me of being a misogynist.

She also said -- goddamn it, this really upset me. She said

this in public, at Emory University (in Atlanta), after a lecture. Somebody asked her who her favorite authors in science fiction were - this was reported to me by Michael Bishop - she says she liked Philip K. Dick's writing, but (laughs) she says, he seems to be spiraling into himself and trying to resolve probably unresolvable metaphysical problems, and is slowly going crazy in Santa Ana, California.

Well, I thought I'd answer that -- I was stung by that "slowly going crazy in Santa Ana, California" and I thought it sounds like the title of an Euripedes play, "Iphigenia in Aulis," going crazy in Santa Ana, California.

At first I was going to say some wiseass thing, like I can go crazy anywhere, Santa Ana has nothing to do with it, and then hang myself like Oscar Wilde did at that trial, you know, he made one smartass remark and wound up in Reading Gaol. So I thought, no, I won't say the smartass thing.

I wrote an open letter to Ursula LeGuin and I sent it to Dick Geis' fanzine, **Science Fiction Review.** And being highly reputable Geis sent it to Ursula. I had written her directly as well, but I hadn't mentioned the (open) letter, so I was guilty (on that point), I guess.

But I said, first of all, do we now have a criterion of what metaphysical problems are resolvable and what are not? Have we now (laughing) drawn up a list of approved problems to work on, and forbidden problems to work on? I said, even if they're insoluable, even if they cannot be solved, perhaps just the pursuit of them in itself is meritorious.

And then I tackled the "going crazy in Santa Ana" thing. I said, Ursula, in my previous book **(A Scanner Darkly)** my protagonist was a narc. Do you suppose that I am also a narcotics agent? Like my protagonist in **VALIS** is crazy, therefore the author's crazy. You see, this would make Agatha Christie a mass murderess (chuckling).

The thing she objected to, the hatred of women -- or as she said, the women are hateful. I guess there's a difference. She said the women were hateful, death-dealing and hateful. And I wrote in my letter, I said the novel **VALIS** is a picaresque novel, which it is -- a loose structure, the vernacular, the first person. In a picaresque novel all the characters are picaroons, they're all rogues. This is how you write a picaresque novel.

And I said that I was tired of the academic idea - this was a sharp dig on my part - I was tired of the academic community and its standards. She said that one of the things that bothered her was my self-portraits in the novel, that I had failed to show the value of art, and the value of the artist. And I said that the only value was in the work, in the novel, not in me. As a person I'm no better than somebody who drives a bus, or who repairs cars. The work is of value, but not me. I don't claim any special status for being a writer.

Then I got to thinking about that later. I thought, perhaps I'm wrong and Ursula's right. Then I got to thinking about everything that Ursula said. Because I really respect Ursula. To me, Ursula is an eminently sane person. I thought, "Shit! Ursula thinks I'm nuts." Perhaps I am (laughs), goddamn, you know.

Well then I'm talking to my agent about that. He says, "Phil!," he says, "Ursula has not read the sequel to **VALIS,** which is coming out in a month or so. In it the women are very favorable and unhateful, they're loving and tender and kind. All Ursula had to do was to wait till the sequel came out. The novel, **Divine Invasion,** is conventionally structured -- you've gone back to a conventional structure, obviously you're not nuts. All she had to do was to wait for the sequel."

* * * * *

10-21-81

GR: You've had an up and down relationship with Ursula LeGuin. You must have met her --
PKD: I have never met Ursula, no, I've never seen her. I've talked to her on the phone, I've corresponded with her many times. It was Ursula who recommended to the Vancouver people that I go up there as their Guest of Honor for the 2nd Vancouver Con (in 1972). She had been the first Guest of Honor the first year. I appreciated that and I like her writing very much. And, uh -- (long pause) the least I can do is to keep in contact with her since (with light irony) she's done so much for me.
GR: She did write that highly favorable piece about you a few years ago.
PKD: In **The New Republic,** yeah. ("Science Fiction as Prophesy," Oct. 30, 1976). I tell you, the word "prophesy" is spelled wrong in the headline. She didn't write the headline, somebody else did.
GR: That novel of hers they did a PBS movie of recently --
PKD: Yeah, **The Lathe of Heaven** (book, 1971, film 1980).
GR: That was really very like one of your novels, as opposed to the others things of hers I've read. (It deals with an alienated young man in a dreary future whose dreams affect reality, altering it under people's feet as in several of Phil's novels. The friendly alien who serves as the boy's spiritual advisor seems a cousin to such Dickian aliens as Lord Running Clam, the "telepathic Ganymedian slime mould" in **Game Players of Titan,** as well).
PKD: Yeah, well, you know what I did -- I tried to find out if she'd read **Ubik** when she wrote that. I wrote and asked her and she did not answer. It was my impression from reading **The Lathe of Heaven** that she'd read **Ubik.**
GR: It's a really Dick-influenced book.
PKD: Yeah, I know. I know. I was able to date when she

wrote it 'cause she sent me an autographed copy when it first came out. She may very well have read **Ubik** and was influenced by my writing. In that case why not tell me? She didn't steal it. I'd like to think I influenced a major writer -- it would be a shot for me. I get a buzz off it, thinking that I influenced Ursula LeGuin.

But she didn't answer that question, although I put it to her point blank. I said, "Had you read **Ubik** when you wrote **Lathe of Heaven?**" But then Ursula a lot of times doesn't answer because Ursula is very busy.

* * * * *

(The Dick-LeGuin correspondence, dated in February 1981, was published in **Science Fiction Review** #39, Summer 1981. In it Phil filled out what he said to me above in more detail.

(It should be noted, in fairness to Ms. LeGuin, that Phil does quote Bishop in the **SFR** letter as saying LeGuin did note at Emory University that she had "the utmost admiration for the work of Philip K. Dick" and that he had "been shamefully ignored critically in this country." LeGuin had indeed been a sincere champion of Phil's work for many years at the time of this incident, and as she notes below "Phil was awfully sensitive" to criticism. Elsewhere in this book you will find his sharp settling of scores with critics and colleagues, over offenses decades old.

(However -- these offenses are not imaginary, and as near as I can judge, Phil is usually right. His sensitivity is part of the same personality that held "a tremendous trust in strangers" and extended a sincere love to the world and everyone in it. He was, as Harlan Ellison noted in his obituary (see **Foundation** 27, February 1983), shamefully used and ripped-off by many who were close to him, at least in his 1970-72 "outlaw" period. I must however register dissent from Ellison's view that Phil was "paranoid, poor, and delusional." Right to the end of his life, no matter how extreme his statements, Phil Dick retained "that inner core of love" (Afterword, **The Golden Man**) he so prized.

(I solicited Ursula LeGuin's comments on the facts of **The Lathe of Heaven** issue. She graciously agreed to respond and I print her letter here:)

February 1, 1984

Dear Gregg Rickman,

While I was reading the stuff you sent I kept thinking about a line in a song, I can't remember if it's Willie Nelson or Waylon, "I've always been crazy, it kept me from going insane" -- that's the only kind of crazy Phil ever was!

I have no idea why I didn't answer Phil's question which he says he asked point blank, "Had you read **Ubik** when you wrote "**Lathe of Heaven?**" -- I guess because I thought he knew, from previous correspondence, that I had read everything he had written that I could get hold of, and reread it. **Ubik** wasn't and still isn't one of my favorites, maybe I was afraid to say anything in case that showed, somehow. Phil was awfully sensitive (as this damned thing I said, one sentence in a Q-and-A session in Atlanta, reported - how accurately I don't know - by Michael Bishop, apparently undid any trust Phil had in me, all the admiration for his work that I had tried to express to him in letters, in reviews, and whenever I was asked who's the best sf writer....all blown away & wasted!). I wonder why he picked on **Ubik** as the one that influenced me in **Lathe.** It was more his whole way of going at a novel that influenced me -- not any one of his novels. The way he wrote just set my mind free. Still does.

I have loaned out my copy of the **Golden Man** collection where the anti-abortion story is so I can't give you the title. That's the one that scared me. I can understand people against the idea that women have a right to abort un unwanted conception, but there were real weird things in that story -- for instance, it did not seem to have occurred to Phil that some aborted fetuses are female. It was an act of aggression by women against **men,** to him, in that story. Other things he wrote at that time seemed to echo this opinion. It seemed both hateful and crazy to me then; still does. But it was evidently Phil being crazy to keep from going insane. Because he soared up out of that stuff with **Timothy Archer,** which maybe is the purest work of genius he ever gave us. What do us poor jerks on the ground do with people like Phil? Love and admire and know we'll never fully understand - and grieve over misunderstandings.

If any of this stuff in this letter is useful to you, please use as you see fit, just saying that it's from a letter to you, which keeps it informal.

All good wishes,

Ursula LeGuin

* * * * *

(I never did quiz Phil on feminism or his opinions on abortion. In his 1980 story notes to "The Pre-Persons" in **The Golden Man** collection he stood by the message of that story, which involves a future society in which children are "pre-persons" until the age of 12, able to be "aborted" by dissatisfied parents at any time. What the story picks up on of course is the notion that fetuses are not human beings until birth, a tenet of the "freedom of choice" movement. The many other issues raised by the abortion controversy slide by; what Phil picked up on beyond the topic of abortion is the awful helplessness of children in any situation. Phil characteristically is on the side of those without a voice.

(All of this is tied in with Phil's lifelong of stormy relationships with women. In the other volumes of this series Phil's painful childhood and the impact on him of the death in infancy of his twin sister will come clear. It was pain he dealt with intelligently and clearly, but it was still very great pain.

(Ursula LeGuin is a very fine writer, but I feel she is not at Phil's level of achievement, or "genius" if you will, simply because she is so "sane" and level-headed. Phil through the pain he suffered in his life was able to take on that of the world, and through his great intelligence and talent able to communicate it in his art. His incredible imagination and saving sense of humor are also key elements of his art, but secondary to his love.

(It is to Ursula LeGuin's great credit that she recognized Phil's special genius and helped bring it to the wider world's attention. And as he will see in Phil's discussion of his Timothy Archer book, which she likes so much, Ursula LeGuin played a key role in "feminizing" it).

* * * * *

PART THREE
The Novels One by One

CHAPTER 16
Self-Denial
"Kindly Death"
Ace Books

9-30-81

(We spoke of his trouble with the **Blade Runner** people, with a recent encounter with a woman "who harrangued me for six hours" - he commented that "this was better than marriage; the abuse without the sex" - and of his rough time in 1972 at the drug rehabilitation center in Canada. At this point I suggested --)

GR: Let's talk about something you have good memories of, like Ace Books.
PKD: (explosive laugh) Let me get something. (Goes to refrigerator for drinks.)

I am now in a position of forced self-denial. I'm into forced self-denial. I can't drink, I'm not supposed to eat hardly anything, I'm supposed to lose a lot of weight -- (As Phil was so thin at this time, down quite a bit from the burliness of his earlier photographs, this talk however jovial must have registered as dangerous somehow. At this point there was a loud pop from his opening of a soft-drink can).

I shot myself. The sound you heard was me shooting myself. (laughs) No, I'm opening a can of Orange Crush. I have to keep eating right, my blood pressure being so high. So I paid the doctor back by eating a lot of potato chips with a lot of salt on them. So my blood pressure would stay the same and they would say I guess he died, let him go back to eating pizza.

It did help (the diet). My blood pressure is now normal. I don't get to do anything. I can't smoke. Charles Platt even told me drinking these Orange Crushes is bad, it dilates the capillaries in your stomach. It's just terrible man, I'll tell you, you can't walk around without encountering death. "Kindly death," as Emily Dickinson says, "is lurking everywhere."

I became convinced I was going to die after I finished this last novel (**The Transmigration of Timothy Archer**). I don't know why I became convinced I was going to die, this is really mysterious, but probably I guess it was because I was writing about three friends of mine who died.

Oh, Ace Books. And then I remember (your question). Bizarre. I guess I immediately left the room and when I got back I started talking about something else. (laughs) I would rather talk about my dead friends than talk about

Ace Books. Does that tell you anything?

What did you want to know about Ace Books? I'll tell you everything. I'm a gold mine of information.

GR: I've got a few pages of questions here.

PKD: Good. That will stop me from rambling. Telling stories about the Civil War. (laughs) How I fought gallantly, and underpaid.

GR: I wanted to go over each of your books.

PKD: Oh, Christ! What a tribulation.

GR: And have you comment on them individually.

PKD: Oh, to keep me on the track.

GR: Well, if you want to talk about Timothy Archer awhile --

PKD: Well, I want to plug my new book, see. This is clever of me. This is really a way of promoting my new novel.

GR: I'll buy a copy of it.

PKD: Your interview is going to be published and everyone who reads it is going to buy a copy. I don't care if you buy a copy, I'll give you a copy. I want your readers to buy a copy. Your manifold readers. So, fire one at me.

GR: I figure we'd start with **Solar Lottery** (1955), and work our way forward.

PKD: Oh, Gahhhd!

* * * * *

CHAPTER 17
The Early Novels:
Solar Lottery
The World Jones Made
The Cosmic Puppets

9-30-81

PKD: (Solar Lottery) was my first novel. Not it wasn't, it was my first published novel. Yeah, I had written a bunch before that. It was my first science fiction novel. I had written unpublished literary - allegedly literary, what I thought was literary - novels.

When I wrote **Solar Lottery,** I modeled it on (A.E.) van Vogt, and I modeled it deliberately on van Vogt, and I have no shame, because he was my hero as a writer and as a person. I wrote a van Vogtian novel. I was not an original writer at that time. I was a very derivative type of writer. I had heroes, and I tried to write like they wrote. He was my **idee fixe** as far as a writer.

So it does resemble a van Vogt novel, which Damon Knight pointed out. When you read it now -- when Tom Disch did the Gregg Press novel, he really couldn't see anything good in this novel (Disch wrote the introduction to the Gregg Press hardcover edition of **Solar Lottery** in 1976).

But Tom is forgetting the time in which it was written... 1954. Well, shit! There was nothing good then. There was one novel, one science fiction novel which had been written that was good. And that was (Alfred) Bester's **The Demolished Man** (1952). And I cribbed from that, the Telepathic Corps.

I mean Disch doesn't have to live those pulp years. It's really easy, in the late '70s and early '80s, to talk about quality. But if he thinks tht he could sell a quality science fiction novel in 1954, he doesn't realize that there was one market and one maket only, and that was Ace Books. And that books were "Doubles," two novels for 35¢. And that you had no latitude. It had to be 6,000 lines and it had to be an adventure novel. There **was** no latitude. You were told exactly what to write. And if we didn't write it for Don Wollheim (science fiction editor at Ace Books), we didn't sell it.

I really cannot take responsibility for the state of the art. Science fiction was rapidly devolving into very poor stuff. By 1959 the total readership had shrunk to 100,000. And when you consider that **Solar Lottery** has sold over 300,000 copies you realize what a commercial success it was. The readership wasn't even there for **Solar Lottery,** and it sold very well.

I'm very defensive about **Solar Lottery.** In terms of the field at the time it was a hell of a good novel. And Damon Knight saw it as what he called an architectural plot in the structure. (See Knight's **In Search of Wonder,** 1967, for his review). But in relationship with later stuff, it sucks. But I was a novice.

I'm shouting. I'm becoming hysterical. (laughs) I'm defending my first novel. (Kurt) Vonnegut's first novel, **Player Piano** (1952), was a masterpiece, and mine wasn't. He's smarter than me.

* * * * *

GR: The World Jones Made (1956).
PKD: Ah! **The World Jones Made.** I read that recently. Now that was an interesting book, because there I tried to tranfer some elements from my quality or literary novels to it. And interestingly enough, although it has not been as successful, and probably is not as good, it's a little more experimental, it's a little more original, than **Solar Lottery.** I did try some idiosyncratic things in it. When you read it over you find a little more character development, it's a little more sophisticated in terms of the characterization. The quality isn't as good, but the characterization is better.

Interestingly enough, it deals with drugs. And we're talking an awfully early novel to deal with drugs. Long before there was a drug subculture. Isn't that interesting, a book that was written in '55 dealing with a drug addict? I knew so little about drugs that I had them taking heroin in capsule form. That's how little I knew. I didn't know you shot heroin. He picks up two capsules of heroin.

And yet I already saw drugs as the coming thing.

* * * * *

GR: Who is Eph Konigsberg? **The World Jones Made** is dedicated to him.

PKD: He's just some fan I met years ago. He gave me that idea about the phenotypes. And I told him that if I did a book on it I'd dedicate the book to him. And I did...I met him once, years later, at a bar, I think in '64 in Oakland at the Worldcon there. He thanked me. I don't think he was very impressed by the book.

GR: Phenotypes are the artificially created aliens (bred from human stock for life on other planets)?

PKD: I have no idea, man. It's a real word and there really are such things as phenotypes, and I knew what it was when I wrote the book. In the book, it's the people they breed for survival on other planets, in other atmospheres, in other gravities.

It would now be called recombinant genetic engineering... That's intresting, come to think of it, that suddenly it's now a real thing that they are really able to do. So they breed them in an artificial environment which duplicates the environment of another planet until they're viable in that environment. So now they're alien to earth. That's not a bad idea!

* * * * *

GR: The Cosmic Puppets (1957).

PKD: Well, that's certainly the greatest fantasy novel ever written. What I was trying to do, I had read every fantasy published in **Unknown Worlds,** which was no longer published when I started writing. So one day I decided, I wonder if I could write a fantasy novel that if **Unknown Worlds** were still in print would be good enough for them to buy.

So I wrote **Cosmic Puppets,** which was originally called "A Glass of Darkness." Tony Boucher did like it, and I was convinced that had that magazine still existed, they would probably have purchased it. But it was a deliberate attempt on my part to see if I could do what people like Clive Cartmill would have done, Heinlein had done, Padget (Lewis Padget, the pseudonym of Henry Kuttner and C.L. Moore), all those people.

It was a tour-de-force in a way. Because I was writing a fantasy novel for a publication that I loved, which no longer existed. I sold it to **Satellite** (magazine, in 1956), and then Don Wollheim picked that up. But I enjoy it. I enjoyed writing it, and I enjoy reading it.

GR: I like it very much. But it's interesting that at the end, with normalcy restored to this little town that had been occupied for twenty years, and kept a sleepy backwater, the triumph of good is represented by the springing into place of shiny shops full of fancy appliances. There isn't the irony that you later developed.

PKD: That's true. There were certain conventional elements in it.

What's interesting in this is, without my intending this, in order to write it I had to do some research into religion. Into Zoroastrianism. And this turned out to be a turning point in my life. Because although I researched Zoroastrinism simply to write a novel, I found that once I had studied a dualistic, bitheistic religion, it was very hard for me to go back to monotheism after that. (The novel deals with the duel between the two gods of Zoroastrianism for control of the small town). I think that once I got the hang of bitheism it was hard to drop it after I had finished reading it.

So it had influenced me spiritually, theologically, religiously, whatever the word is, the amount of research that I did. That had not been my intention.

GR: Why (after publication in 1957) was **The Cosmic Puppets** never been reprinted?

PKD: I have a contract with Berkley to bring that out, but it's a tie-in contract that requires me to revise **Unteleported**

Man (1966), but I can't get back into that space of **The Unteleported Man** to rewrite it...

I originally conceived of myself as a fantasy writer (many of Phil's early stories are in fact fantasies) ...I would have starved to death writing that kind of stuff. But I loved that kind of fantasy myself. Of course, now there's this tremendous market for fantasy. (But) I no longer understand fantasy. I've lost the knowledge.
(**The Cosmic Puppets** was finally reprinted in 1983).

* * * * *

CHAPTER 18
The Early Novels:
The Man Who Japed
Eye in the Sky
Marxism / Semi-Reality
Race / An Old Black Man

9-30-81

GR: The Man Who Japed (1956).
PKD: Wollheim said that was the worst of them all. That's how he put it. They were all bad, and it was a question of which was the worst. He said, I consider it the weakest of them all.

That was my attempt to introduce humor into the science

fiction novel. It was a very inadequate book, there is no doubt about it. But it does have, for the first time, my sense of humor is beginning to show up in a novel. And I'm beginning not to take myself quite so seriously. It's a little more balanced. A lot of the humor that comes later in my writing, which is successful, can be seen in an early form in **The Man Who Japed.** The guy finding the head when he goes to buy a pie in the automat. That kind of thing.

Tony Boucher reviewed it and said it had one good scene. I think it was that scene on television. They're justifying their actions and finally realize they're justifying cannibalism. (laughs) I still think that's funny.

Okay, I wrote a funny book and it wasn't a heavyweight book, it was a lightweight book. And another thing, that MOREC (the "Moral Reclamation" dictatorship that rules Earth), that was based on what I'd read about Communist China, the incredible puritanical strain that was showing up in Communist China. I based it on that block ward thing in China, every block had its political commissar. Now, the interesting thing is that someone who understands that element in **Man Who Japed** would never make the error of thinkinng that I was a Communist or a Marxist. Because that is a very, very sincere attempt to show the very dangerous trends in Communism, the Communist state. And I think a lot of the people who have assumed that I am a Marxist -- which, by the way, Disch assumes. He calls me the only Marxist science fiction writer there is.

That's not true. I am not a Marxist. And that book should really have clued anybody in who was really astute. What he's basing that statement on - and it's not just Tom Disch who thinks that, a lot of people have thought I'm a Marxist - is that I grew up in Berkeley, and there's kind of a quasi-Marxist quality in a lot of my writing. Because I will attack the industrial establishment with certain slogans that are associated with Marxism. Everybody in Berkeley talked that way, it's the Berkeley patois. We talked about the "fascists" and we talked about the "capitalists" and so on, and that's the way people talked there. And that doesn't mean they're Marxists. It's the area. It was then and it is now.

Because Berkeley had been in the '30s the absolute capital of Communism in the western part of the United States. In the '30s there was a real Communist community in Berkeley. Now, I was just a child then, but even as a child I was exposed to that. I had a babysitter who was a Party member. And they were openly Party members. That's the difference. In the '30s people were openly Party members. Prominent people.

It was like belonging to the Democratic Party in the '30s. I said to my mother once, "Mom, how come my babysitter continually tells me about life in the Soviet Union and how great it is?" Well, she said, she's a member of the Communist Party. That's an interesting milieu, isn't it? And every day my babysitter would tell me about the tractor factory at Stalingrad, the heroic workers.

GR: This comes out in **Eye in the Sky** (1957), the fantasy world of the guy who's a Communist.

PKD: Yeah, yeah. That's another thing that indicates that I can't really be said honestly to be a Communist. I parodied and savagely attacked them in **Eye in the Sky.** And Poul Anderson noticed that. Poul said he thought that part where the Communist slogans fall out of the sky, fiery symbols fall from the heavens, and set fire to somebody's house was one of the funniest things he had ever read.

Eye in the Sky was not only openly attacking the McCarthy witch hunts, because that was written during the McCarthy witch hunt period, but I was also attacking Communism too. I was attacking them both. So I don't **understand** this business (of saying I'm a Marxist).

GR: One of the things that runs all through your work,

especially in the early '60s to jump ahead a bit, and also in your early stories is a satire of the Cold War. For instance, just yesterday I read an early short story of yours, "Foster, You're Dead" (1955). (A small boy is only happy when underground in his parents' fall-out shelter, and nags his father to buy increasingly newer models).

PKD: Yes, yes. Well, see that's the thing. If you get these people who assume there's two sides, the Communist side and the "Free World," which is how they say it (to them that's it). But I have always maintained that there are more than two sides to this matter. We're not limited to choosing between Catholics and Communists; there are all kinds of alternative solutions.

And also people confuse -- I remember once this teacher I had in high school said, you have a choice between communism and democracy. And I immediately leapt up and said, "No, no, it's capitalism and communism. Democracy and fascism." I said you're confusing an economic system with a political system. And he said, you sit down and shut up or I'm giving you an F.

That's the thing. In many ways I was an anti-capitalist, but that didn't make me a Marxist. I was very, very suspicious, terribly suspicious of totalitarian states, whether right or left wing. I would say the real enemy, the enemy which to me is the paradigm of evil, is the totalitarian state, and it can be religious, it can be left wing, it can be right wing. I was just horrified at what I saw during the Eisenhower period in this country, at what appeared to me to be a great movement toward a totalitarian state in the United States. A right wing totalitarian state. Where anybody who is a dissenter is labeled as a traitor. That is of course the mark of a totalitarian society, when any dissent is regarded as treason.

The moment you know dissent is regarded as treason, you know right away you've got totalitarianism, and then it's incumbent on you to dissent your ass off. Just protest everything. At that point, a really moral person, once he notices that trend, of the equating of dissent and treason, has a moral obligation to oppose the authorities.

My real stance was opposing authority. And I opposed the Communist authorities as much as I opposed the American authorities. I had a girlfriend in Berkeley who was a member of the Communist Party. And I caused her such trouble that they forbade her to see me anymore. She took me to one meeting and I got up and informed them their analysis of fascism was completely wrong, they had no understanding of fascism. I explained what fascism was. They told me again, like the teachers, to sit down and shut up, and they they told her never to see me again. In fact they even threatened my life. This is incredible. One guy walked me all the way home. He kept talking about (how) I could get strung up if I wasn't careful about what I said, 'cause I sounded like a fascist. It sounded like I was defending fascism. Guys who do that, he said, sometimes wind up hanging from telephone poles.

GR: How about your girlfriend? Did you see her again?

PKD: Yeah, one day, in a restaurant. She walked up, said "hi," and dropped her cigarette into my cup of coffee, and walked away.

People in Berkeley took politics seriously. My favorite trick - I will probably have to pay for this when I die - would appear to inadvertently introduce somebody who was a Trotskyite, a Trot, to a member of the CP, a Stalinist. "Oh Liz, meet my friend John." Without identifying either of them. They'd talk along all right, and then they'd discover that one was a Trotskyist, and one was a Stalinist. And immediately they'd just turn and run frantically, because each of them was in danger of being expelled from his organization, the SWP (Socialist Worker's Party) or the CP. They literally could be expelled if they were seen talking to each other. They were not allowed to do that. I used to love to do that.

And then the hatred. Each of them would seek me out later and say, do you realize what you did, and I'd say "No, I just thought you might like to meet each other. I mean, after all, you're both interested in politics."

GR: Well, let's do **Eye in the Sky.**

PKD: Now there I wrote a book that was a joy to write. That only took me two weeks to write. I just breezed through that. By then I had a command of dialogue. Now, all of a sudden I could write dialogue. I could write funny. I just suddenly made a great breakthrough with **Eye in the Sky.** Wollheim recognized this, and published it as a single, rather than as an Ace Double. The first time he'd ever done that. And he advertised it and everything.

I think the characterization is good, I think the idea is original. Well no, it isn't original. I stole it from Frederic Brown's **What Mad Universe** (1949). I reapplied it. Instead of having one fantasy universe I had a series of competing fantasy, or irreal, universes.

And there of course my preoccupation with irreality, the fradulent universe, begins. That's the origin right there. The idea had occured to me that maybe what we see is not real. That it is somehow -- I don't know what the alternative to "real" is. There are actually several alternatives. Even "unreal" is not the perfect term. There's a state of things being semi-real, which is an interesting concept, something being semi-real. That could tie you up for years, trying to imagine what the **hell** could be meant by "semi-real."

I came across that term recently. I've been reading about Plato, and he regarded the phenomenal world (that perceived by the senses) as semi-real. That would certainly stop conversation for a long time, for people who had not heard that term ever before, didn't know what Plato meant by that. This character says, "By the way, that table is semi-real." You say it's not real, everybody will argue simply that it is real. But if you say it's only semi-real, it's a very puzzling idea.

And I guess I was getting into it without realizing I was getting into a kind of Platonist frame of reference where I regarded the phenomenal world as just semi-real. That it has some existence to it, it's not merely a hallucination. This is something Santayana, the great Indian philosopher, once said: he said don't ever think that the Veil of Maya is like a hallucination. What it is like is a conjuror's trick where the conjuror shows you a rope and convinces you it's a snake. Now there is something there, but it's not what you're convinced it is. That is what Maya is. There is something there, but it is not what it appears to be. Maya can seem to be anything he wants. But to argue what is Maya actually is to miss the point of the whole thing. The question "What is Maya?" is unanswerable. Because Maya be its very definition does not admit to an answer to that question.

I was beginning to deal with this stuff in **Eye in the Sky,** and I loved it. I loved thoughts like this. Plus the idea that each of us lives in a somewhat different world than anybody else. Some people's worlds are more unusual than other people's. For instance the world of a puritanical, middle-aged woman is quite different from the world of, say, a Communist. Well, not completely different.

Well, let's see here. What did I do? A religious bigot, puritanical woman, Communism -- oh, a totally psychotic woman. Joan Reiss. Oh, Jesus. The world of a paranoid. God.

Now, one of my wives read that book, and said you are insane. Only a person who was mentally ill could write something like that. I said, fine, Agatha Christie is a mass murderess then. The same logic. I was able to imagine the different world of the different people.

But that Joan Reiss section, that is scary.

(Among the normal people whose worlds are not entered into) there is a black. In **Solar Lottery** the captain of the space ship is black. That was deliberate on my part, because (Robert) Heinlein had said somewhere that all the races had their place in the future. The blacks would serve the food, you know, and the Chinese would do the laundry, the whites would be in the control room. He had a caste system with a descending order of intelligence, with the blacks at the bottom. I was just furious about that, and I had a black guy be the captain of the space ship. Just as an answer to Heinlein.

Now, by the time I got to **Eye in the Sky,** I had the white guy and the black guy go into partnership at the end, and form a business together. I know today that this seems impossible to believe, but what year is this now? In 1956, when I wrote it, it was **unthinkable** for a black guy and a white guy to go in business together. It **never** happened. Even in Berkeley it never happened. It was like racial intermarriage, where it was illegal in several states. It was unthinkable that a black guy and a white guy would go in business together, because they would then be equals, and that is the climate that existed then. And I got more comments about that in Berkeley than I got on any other aspect of the book.

GR: Favorable?

PKD: Yeah. It was very daring and very progressive of me to do that. To hold that view of the races that early. It was quite daring.

GR: The black guy is not a plaster saint, either. He has real problems because of what he's gone through.

PKD: Oh yeah, right. I had a black friend. The guy who taught me to drive. I was living in a very poor section of Berkeley down in the flatlands, by San Pablo Avenue. A black family moved in across the street, and they busted the block -- block-busting, you know. And nobody would speak to them. But I used to go over and talk. I bought a car and didn't know how to drive it and he had a chauffeur's license. And it's very hard to get a chauffeur's license; you have to be a real good driver, and this guy was really good.

He taught me to drive and it took months, literally, because I was really very bad. Very bad. I mean it, literally months to teach me. And he got nothing back. He wouldn't accept a dime. When I got my license I got him some western novels - he liked to read western novels - a bottle of some beer for him, and a couple of little things, and he and his wife wrote me and my wife a thank you card as if **they** were in **our** debt. He had spent months with me. It's just incredible, this guy.

And when my wife was in the car, he would not sit in the front seat. He would always sit in the back. He was going to teach her to drive, but he couldn't stand the stress of being in the same car with a white woman. He finally said, I can't do it, I can't be in the car with her. He wouldn't even come into my house; can you imagine that? He would sit on (my) front porch, and drink beer. In celebration of my license I got some beer, and invited him and his wife over, and he would sit on the porch and drink, but he would not come into the house. This was in Berkeley too, can you dig? That's how bad the (racial) relationships were.

He was a very fine man. And his father, who was very elderly, would sit out on the front in a chair. And when the kid who delivered the shopping news would come along, the kid would throw it right at this old black, to try and hit him. And he did it once, but he missed and it shalommed off the wall. He threw as hard as he could, I saw him. The black man would never flinch or move or even show that he noticed. The kid threw my shopping news on the porch and I leaped out the door, grabbed it and said, "You do that one more time, you little fucker, and I'll kill you." I was just furious. And the black guy never moved a muscle. But he saw this all happen. An old, old black man.

CHAPTER 19
The Early Novels:
Time Out of Joint
Gnosticism / The Tao
Vulcan's Hammer
Dr. Futurity
Ray Bradbury

9-30-81

GR: (We'd been talking about his marital problems). Well, let's get back to fiction. Sometimes fiction is more pleasant than real life.

PKD: Except my fiction isn't.

    Time Out of Joint (1958). Now that was a really perilous gamble on my part to write because there was no chance that Donald Wollheim would buy **Time Out of Joint.** That meant that I could not possibly sell it as a science fiction novel. It was bought by Lippincott as a "novel of menace." I only got 750 bucks for it. It was really a risky thing to do.

But there again we are dealing with fake reality and I had become obsessed with the idea of fake reality. I was just fascinated with the idea. So that's a pivotal book in terms of my career. It was my first hardcover sale, and it was the first novel I wrote in which the entire world is fake. You find yourself in it when you pick up the book and turn to page one. The world that you are reading about does not exist. And this was to be essentially the premise of my entire corpus of writing, really. This is my underlying premise. And this is that the world that we experience is not the real world. It's as simple as that. The phenomenal world is not the real world, it's something other than the real world. It's either semi-real, or some kind of forgery.

This is Gnosticism. One of the Gnostics wrote about "the illusory creator and his non-real universe," which is a very startling idea. I guess it's logical that an illusory creator would create an irreal universe. But what in hell are we talking about here? Are we talking about anything at all? What characteristics could something that doesn't exist have? It's enough to keep you awake at night.

It's like I read in the introduction to my **I Ching,** the statement that Westerners tend to confuse that which exists as that which is real. (This belief) bipolarizes what is real and what exists, which is an incredible thing. Conceptually, we can't bipolarize what is real from what exists. But the Tao does not exist. Yet it exerts an inexorable influence on reality.

The Tao is nothing, yet it tugs eternally at reality, shaping it as the potter shapes the clay. How can something that doesn't exist do that? It's like a linguistic problem, it's like we're dealing with a problem in semantics. I define anything which is capable of perturbing and shaping and tugging reality as itself possessing of some kind of reality.

I don't see how it can be called "nothing." I don't understand then what the word "nothing" signifies. If you take a magnetic field that shapes iron filings into a pattern, that magnetic field is intangible, but it's real. It does exist.

I think it's the semantics....In antiquity, it was so difficult for the Greeks to conceive of abstractions as incorporeal, that the Pythagoreans who believed that number was the basis of reality believed that numbers were physical objects. That "four" was four objects arranged in a pattern, like four pebbles, for example. "Three" would be a triangle. "Four" would be a square. They actually envisioned them as being substantial objects, like Democritean atoms, which were like hard little objects. Even numbers were like hard little objects to them.

They really were not able to fully abstract. This is one of the most profound things I've learned in reading early Greek philosophy, was that they literally could not abstract completely. For instance, the Stoics belief in the **logos** -- they believed that the **logos** had a physical presence. It permeated reality like a drop of wine in the ocean. It was very subtle, but it was nevertheless corporeal. It had a material existence. That was the closest they could come to conceiving of a full abstraction.

I could talk about this for hours. This is my **raison d'etre,** this particular subject.

* * * * *

GR: (While Phil was trying to get his literary novels published, there were two more science fiction novels printed to finish off the First Period)...**Vulcan's Hammer** (1960)?
PKD: That was just a quickie to make some money. That was a rewrite of a novelette. (Published under that name in

Future magazine, 1956).

We needed money and I had stopped writing pretty much. That was in '59 when a lot of the science fiction field had collapsed. A lot of writers were leaving the field. The readership had shrunk to 100,000. There was no money to be made at all. It was a marketing problem. The standards were low, the pay was low. All the magazines had collapsed, save **Galaxy, Astounding,** and **F&SF**.

There was no market for stories, there was no market for novels and we just en masse gave up. I gave up and went into jewelry (he built a shop for his wife, Anne, to handcraft jewelry in).

GR: I regard **Vulcan's Hammer** as your weakest book.

PKD: Of course it's my weakest book. It's symptomatic of what was going on.

Dr. Futurity (1960) -- Well that's just worthless. Again, it's just an attempt to turn out a novel to make some money. It was the state of the art at that time. That was the state at which science fiction was at at that point.

GR: It's clever. The time paradoxes are good.

PKD: Yeah, but we're talking about a period of very small readership, very conventional ideas, no technique. No really good writers were coming into the field. We weren't getting any new blood. The great writers of the past were either dying or repeating themselves. The failure of new blood was central of this problem.

Because why should they come into a field in which there's no market, no pay, no prestige. What would be the motivation to come in? The only one was (Kurt) Vonnegut, that was the only one. Bradbury was selling slicks, so he was appealing to a different market. He'd found that formula for nostalgia and stuff, Americana.

Bradbury is a great writer. But essentially Bradbury is rehashing a lot of the Walt Whitman "Leaves of Grass" sort of thing. "I hear America singing," "I sing the body electric," it's all that kind of thing. Bradbury can wax lyrical in heroic couplets about Disneyland. He can write in heroic couplets like Dryden.

* * * * *

CHAPTER 20
The Literary Novels
Confessions of a Crap Artist
Craftsmen, Intellectuals, Salesmen

4-22-81

GR: It is my understanding that you quit writing for a year in 1960-61 out of frustration that your best books weren't being printed -- your mainstream, literary novels, like **Confessions of a Crap Artist.** Did you have other mainstream novels you were trying to sell?
PKD: Would you believe 13? Some as long as 600 pages. Slave labor.

It was really something. There's eleven of those manuscripts still in existence...**Confessions of a Crap Artist** was virtually the last one, I only wrote one after (it). And when I wrote that I was influenced by Nathaniel West. I had read all of Nathanial West, which is real easy as he only wrote four books.

But there is no evidence of a Nathaniel West influence on the book when you read it. I don't know what made me think I was under the Nathaniel West influence.

Harcourt Brace liked it enough. They gave me $500 just as a bonus, without a contract or anything, for having written it. But they didn't buy it. They said, this will be an incentive to write another one. Maybe we'll buy the next one.

Well, the next one I wrote they didn't buy, and that was it. I never wrote any more, except the one I'm working on now. I shouldn't be thinking back to those 13. Christ!

Most of those were written around the time I started selling, like 1951, '52, '53. Most of them are really fairly early.

* * * * *

9-30-81

GR: In **Do Androids Dream,** the character of Jack Isidore recurs (somewhat altered), from **Confessions.**
PKD: I was cannibalizing **Confessions** because I didn't expect it ever to be published. And I liked Jack Isidore (the perceptive idiot) as a character.

* * * * *

(**Confessions** is) autobiographical....(It) finally saw print, although as you know only in a 5,000 copy edition (printed in a limited edition by Paul Williams' Entwhistle Books in

1975, it was released as a mass-market paperback in late 1982). But I think it's a good book. I think it's a hell of a good book. And I think that the one I wrote afterwards is a hell of a good book. And my agent has it now and it's circulating.

That's **The Man Whose Teeth Were All Exactly Alike** (completed 1960). (**Man Whose Teeth** was published in May 1984 by Mark Ziesling. Two more of Phil Dick's literary novels have also found publishers since his death: **In Milton Lumky Territory,** from David Hartwell's Dragon Press, and **Puttering About in a Small Land,** by Academy Chicago. For more information on these editions, see the PKDS **Newsletter**).

I had plundered it for **Penultimate Truth**, but there's enough in the original novel that it can still be published. And I'm hoping very much that it will sell. I read it over and I liked it a lot. I was reading the others and I didn't care for the others at all. But **The Man Whose Teeth** is really a very well written book.

(Note: the "plundering" Phil refers to is probably the concept of the Neanderthal-like "Chuppers" in **The Simulacra,** "the Men Whose Teeth Were All Exactly Alike" being a colony of Neanderthal-like throwbacks in the earlier novel. For the record, of the three unpublished Dick novels I have read, I prefer **Mary and the Giant** to **Teeth,** with the very early **Gather Yourselves Together** a distinct third.)

GR: Confessions is very well written.

PKD: Well, I went on and wrote one more, which is at least as good. I'd like to sell it. I don't care about making any money. My agent said if he sold it he could only make a thousand bucks on it, which is nothing to me. That's all right.

GR: As long as we're on the subject I'll go over the list of your unpublished novels. **Mary and the Giant?**

PKD: It's a retelling of the Don Giovanni story, an older man is seduced by a young woman. The girl destroys him. It retells Mozart's Don Giovanni. (It was written in) the early '50s.

Gather Yourselves Together -- That's an early novel. I don't remember anything about that. I can't give you word one about that except that it's another early one and I'm sure it's unpublishable. (The novel is set in China in an isolated factory after the departure of the Nationalists. The Western caretakers of the factory kill time and reminisce about their earlier lives in flashback as they await the arrival of the Communists. Unlike the poignant and at times savagely funny **Mary and the Giant** the writing in this one is a bit stiff, though not without its moments).

Puttering About in a Small Land -- Now that wasn't half bad. The intent was good. It starts with a theme that has been varied on in my later writing, about a man who is not as educated as his wife. It's the story of a guy who is essentially an artisan, a craftsman, a guy who repairs TV sets. His wife is a college graduate, much more educated than him. It's a story of how eventually her economic ambitios and her social ambitions and her education undermine his own respect for himself until finally, like Swann in **Memories of Things Past,** his self-confidence is so undermined that he's destroyed as a person.

...Well I've always had a great regard for men who worked with their hands. Craftsmen as it were. I have a little anti-intellectualism. I guess it's a reaction to Berkeley with their intellectuality. I guess it's an element in me where I loathe snobbery, I loathe elitism, and I loathe intellectuals who feel they're superior because they're highly educated. When I went to Berkeley, when I went to UC Cal., I started running into those people, and I just loathed them for feeling superior because of their damned degrees, their damned classes and their snobbery. That's one reason I dropped out of Cal. I identified with the TV repairmen that I knew. Guys with no degrees, humane, intelligent and warm. Good guys. And I saw how they were looked upon by the intellectual intelligencia and I identified **against** the intelligencia. A very powerful trait in me is an anti-elitism, a kind of Jacksonian populism. I'm not a Know-Nothing, of course.

In Milton Lumky Territory -- that's about a salesman, by and large a rehash of Arthur Miller's **Death of a Salesman,** which had influenced me enormously ideologically. The whole thing "attention must be paid to this man," that fitted my ideology exactly, that was completely the way I felt. There was great dignity in this salesman, there was great dignity in his aging and suffering and death. I was really young then, and I was terribly aware of the pain that people felt when they began to get old. I would see friends of mine who were TV repairmen begin to get old, and how they suffered when some hot shot repairmen would come in. I would see the pressure this put them under, to keep up, always keep up, always keep up. And I was very concerned about this and I was just in my 20s. I would see these men in their 50s and 60s and the fear, the terrible fear, and the terrible pressure they'd put on themselves to keep up. The very act of forcing themselves to compete would hasten their own demise. It brought about the very collapse they feared. Because they didn't have the stamina, the strength left, the vitality. The harder they tried to keep up, the more doomed they were. I saw this as tragic, and in the classic sense. The very act of trying to keep up doomed them to fall behind, by hideous paradox.

The Broken Bubble of Thisbe Holt -- I wouldn't even want to describe it. It's just a bad book.

GR: The name "Thisbe Holt" recurs as the name of a character in **The Crack in Space** (1966). (It is "Thisbe Olt" who operates the Golden Door Moments of Bliss whorehouse satellite).

PKD: I just used the name. It's the study of how a woman is degraded. In that book the degradation is of a young woman. All of these are about the same time, early '50s.

They're quite long. The longest is **Voices from the Street** (652 typewritten pages). That's about a man becoming paranoid. So he finally is kiled. He's destroyed by his own paranoia.

GR: Did you try and sell these books?

PKD: Sure. My agent submitted them to every publisher in America. No luck.

(The list of Phil's unpublished novels I was working off of was that of the manuscripts on file at California State University Fullerton. In a letter to Eleanor Dimoff of Harcourt Brace, dated February 1, 1960, Phil discusses his unpublished novels **A Time for George Stavros** and **Nicholas and the Higs** in addition to **The Broken Bubble of Thisbe Holt** and **In Milton Lumky Territory.** It was Harcourt Brace's lack of interest in his projected rewrite of **George Stavros** that probably led as much as anything else to his period of not writing, before he began **Man in the High Castle.** The Dimoff letter was published as a pamphlet by the Philip K. Dick society in 1983).

* * * * *

CHAPTER 21

The Novels of the Early Sixties: The Man in the High Castle / The Multi-Foci Format / A Sequel to High Castle / Nazis / Mussolini and Now Wait For Last Year / The Nature of Evil

9-30-81

GR: That's the end of the First Period, the '50s, ending with your retirement. Why the revival in the 1960s?
PKD: I was miserable not writing. I couldn't live without writing. And when I went back into writing it was a do or die situation. Either I wrote something so outstanding and so revolutionary and so original, or there was no point to

back to writing. There was no point to going back to writing things like **Vulcan's Hammer.**

So if I went back to writing at all, I would have to rise to a level I had never risen to and no one had ever risen to. Or else there was no reason to. I yearned to write and this was pent up in this tremendous desire to write. So when I went back to writing and wrote **The Man in the High Castle** (1962), there was this tremendous reservoir of driving and ideas and strength in me, so it was easy to write. It was very easy to write that book - it required no outline, no plot structure in advance - it just happened. All that time without writing, the book had just built up in me. I was really high.

But, as I say, if you go back in you have to do something really great. It would be pointless, almost nihilistic to go in and write another crap book. So that was voluntary to write a better book, that was something I wanted to do. It's like this literary novel, **The Transmigration of Timothy Archer,** I **wanted** to do that. I did.

I sat down at a cheap little $65 Royal portable typewriter, where the "e" key stuck all the time, alone in a little cabin my wife and I owned. Everyday I'd sit there and write.

GR: What gave you the idea of the book, that the Axis had won World War II?

PKD: I had had that idea for years. That idea had been in the back of my mind for years. I had already done all the research when I was still in Berkeley. I had never been able to figure out how to handle it, until the time of writing it. All of a sudden I figured out how to handle it, and just sat right down and did it.

GR: And it was a great success (it won the Hugo Award in 1963 for Best Novel).

PKD: Yeah, but that was just a fluke. I had no reason to expect it would be a great success. It was bought by a very fine editor, Pete Israel, who was very very good, and he had me make a lot of changes in it which improved it enormously. Very, very substantial changes -- I don't remember what. But they were very laborious for me, involved almost a complete rewriting of the book. He was a quality editor, an excellent editor, He's still around. He's a writer himself.

It was not published as science fiction. He did not regard it as science fiction. It was not what science fiction was perceived to be. Tony Boucher simply said it was a mainstream novel. That is not true, by the way -- it's not a normal mainstream novel. The structure of that novel is based on a novel structure used by the students in the French Department of Tokyo University after World War II. That's an Oriental structure based on a French model. That's not a mainstream structure. That's a structure I worked out based on many diverse sources. Tony later reversed that position, that it was just a mainstream novel with a science fiction premise -- later he told me he considered it a breakthrough novel. He came to view it that way.

GR: You continued using this multiple character, multi-foci format.

PKD: Yeah, I loved that. Since I do not hold there is one reality, I hold that each person has their own, somewhat unique reality, it would be natural for me to use a multiple-foci type thing. That would be for me the only way you could really capture reality would be if you did that. No one person could see enough of reality. That was how I viewed reality. It was almost from a field standpoint.

GR: I read somewhere that you'd sketched out a sequel to **The Man in the High Castle**, but found it too depressing to actually write.

PKD: Yeah. I worked out a plot. I don't have a transcript of it -- I taped it. I did a tape recording of the sequel, the plot outline. I don't have a transcript of it, but I do have the tape. Or maybe it's at the Fullerton Library (the Cal State

Fullerton Special Collections repository of his manuscripts, letters, etc.) But I'll never write it because it is too depressing.

I think it dealt mainly with Reinhard Heydrich. I honestly don't remember. It was '64 (when I did it).

GR: You obviously researched the period quite thoroughly, and your speculations on the alternate history seem acute.

PKD: I considered myself an authority on National Socialism.

GR: You have a lot of Germans in your early '60s books. Hermann Goering is in **The Simulacra.**

PKD: Yes.

GR: Are you German? Is Dick a German name? (I had so speculated in the version of the essay Phil saw).

PKD: No, it's Scotch.

GR: Well, I better fix that.

PKD: I really regarded the National Socialists as an enigmatic matter. (It's) very somber how a thing like that could arise, in a country that provided Goethe, Beethoven, Schiller.

I read Hannah Arendt's book, **The Origins of Totalitarianism,** and it aided me very much in understanding. I did study the National Socialist mind until I felt I could understand the world from their standpoint.

I don't think the true National Socialism has been exported, because the mystic underpinnings of it did not catch on in the world. Some of the political things did. But National Socialism and Fascism are not the same. Mussolini was Fascist, but in no way did he hold the mystical ideas that are associated with Alfred Rosenberg and the other theoreticians who were associated with the National Socialist Party. Hitler and Goebbels and Rosenberg.

I suppose you could adopt the position of moral theoreticians and simply say they were absolutely evil through and through. Essentially a Manichean view. If there is such a thing as absolute evil, it can manifest itself.

I knew a Nazi, later, in '71. A real Nazi, not a Fascist. I got to see into his mind. It's quite different from Fascism. In some ways I was quite an admirer of Mussolini. He's the basis for Gino Molinari in **Now Wait for Last Year** (1966. Molinari is the world dictator who, having made the ghastly mistake of allying Earth with an evil alien race, submits to massive physical suffering as his way of both protecting Earth and doing penance).

I think Mussolini was a very, very great man. But the tragedy for Mussolini was he fell under Hitler's spell. But then so did many others. In a way you can't blame Mussolini for that.

GR: This really helps in an analysis of **Now Wait for Last Year.** You have Mussolini becoming Christ, torturing himself -- and the reason we made an alliance with the Lilistar race was that they looked just like us, and their foes, the reegs, looked like repulsive insects. But of course the ones who don't look like us at all are actually the good side.

PKD: Yes.

GR: I wanted to ask you about that, the Christ figures in your books. I notice you have a figure of Christ on your wall.

PKD: Alleged figure.

GR: Well, a suffering figure who looks like Christ.

PKD: He'll do.

GR: And a cross right next to it. (In fact, Phil's large poster of Christ in agony dominated his living room, although he also had posters of Janis Joplin and a B. Kliban cat along hs walls)

PKD: Yes.

GR: So in Molinari we have a cross between your Christ figures and another of your favorite types of characters, the fat, powerful dictator -- although a Stanton Brose in **Penultimate Truth** is completely evil (and Willis Gram in Our Friends from Frolix 8, more humanized but still evil)

while Molinari is halfway between the extremes.
PKD: Well that stems from my ambivilence about Mussolini. He died such a tragic death (shot and hung upside down with his mistress). What was done to Mussolini, Mussolini never did to his political opponents. He never slaughtered them and hung them head down.
GR: Well, he was a dictator. He went in more towards internal exile and castor oil.
PKD: There is a difference between giving somebody castor oil and giving them Xyclon B. We pass over from a repressive regime to something so monstrous--

If I hadn't read the correspondence between the SS and the baker oven building firm in Germany that built those ovens -- they built ovens for bread. And the SS wrote to all the firms in Germany which had built ovens to make bread, and informed them that they wanted to build ovens to burn up human bodies, and what were the bids on this project, like any commercial project. They got competitive bids.

Not one firm wrote back and said, We don't build ovens to burn bodies. Not one firm. All these people who built ovens knew then, what most Germans did not know. That large numbers of people were being killed, and their bodies were being burned. This is one of the leaks that should have tipped somebody off. Any given firm that got that notice for competitive bidding, should have and probably did know immediately what was happening. None of them leaked the news. All of them gave competitive bids.

It simply cannot be that such is the case and yet indeed it was the case. They actually - Jesus! - bid for that contract. I find this to be the most extraordinary thing I have ever heard.

And it is also very illustrative of the nature of ethics. Ethics may far more involve an abstraction from evil than a commission of good. We tend to regard ethics and morality as motivations to do good, good works. It may be actually more identifiable authentically with a balking and a refusal. Like if the oven company had written back, We don't make ovens to burn bodies. That would have been no act, and yet in way it was, because it would have put them in prison.

To distinguish that one is being asked to do something evil, to perceive this, may be even more fundamental ethically than the commission of a good deed, in the sense of like giving money to charity, you know. I'm sure they all contributed to the Winter Help Fund, which is a Germany charitable organization. They all contributed to the Help Fund, and then turned around and built ovens to burn bodies.

You could bring up this thing with Dow Chemical in making napalm. You could say, Do you know -- you could say to Dow Chemical, Do you know what the napalm is for? Well of course they know what it is for. It's not to kill fish. It's to kill people. Do you know what it's like to be killed by napalm? Well, yes we do, because we invented it. We know what the effects are of being napalmed. Then how can you manufacture and market napalm? -- You see, that's the same thing.

All that is being asked is a refusal. No one is being asked to do anything, merely being asked to refuse to do something they shouldn't do. To balk. I define as human that organism that, which when perceiving a threat to its moral integrity, balks. And therefore shows nothing externally, perhaps. There is no deed to commit, no act to record, but reuses to do something, from some kind of innate perception that this is not done. Fucking napalm...

(Phil Dick has said elsewhere he researched **High Castle** by reading wartime archives kept at UC Berkely in the 1950s. This is where he would have seen SS correspondence with oven manufacturers).

* * * * *

CHAPTER 22
The Novels of the Early Sixties:
"68 Pages a Day"
Martian Time-Slip
"I Had Found My Own Idiom"
The Three Stigmata of Palmer Eldritch

9-30-81

GR: After **High Castle,** you entered an extremely prolific period (from nothing published in 1961, and one novel -- **High Castle** - in 1962, Dick published one novel and five stories in 1963, four novels and ten stories in 1964. Several of the stories formed the core of later novels).
PKD: Well I had found a structure and I just wrote novel

after novel. There's not much to be said regarding any one of them specifically. I had my structure, my multi-foci structure, and I had won the hugo Award for **Man in the High Castle,** so I figured I could sell my stuff now and I just wrote a lot.

GR: But they're quite good. Some of them are very different.

PKD: All I remember is writing 68 pages a day.

GR: Were you on a different typewriter by then?

GR: Were you on a different typewriter by then?

PKD: Electric.

GR: You have nothing to say about **Game Players of Titan** (1963)?

PKD: Not a thing.

GR: The Simulacra (1964)?

PKD: Just another multi-focus novel.

GR: Penultimate Truth (1964)?

PKD: Same thing.

GR: What about **Martian Time-Slip?** (Serialized in 1963 as "All We Marsmen," published as a paperback book in 1964).

PKD: Now there's a story there. **Martian Time-Slip** was my attempt to excalate from **Man in the High Castle** to the next level of quality, complexity, and value. But it was badly received in the marketplace, no hard cover publisher was interested, and it would up selling to Ballantine for $2,000. And it completely deflated me. I felt it was a very good book, a very serious book, and a very important book, and there was no response, the book just disappeared, it didn't sell very many copies. They put my name in real small print. All the headway I had made since **Man in the High Castle,** in terms of marketing, was now gone. And I got very despairing at that point. It was a great blow to me, that **Martian Time-Slip** was not better received. It went unnoticed, it went unreviewed, unnoticed by the critics, by the publishers, and by the readers.

That of course is all changed now. There's over 215,000 copies in print. But at the time there was just no interest in it in the field. It was regarded as science fiction but they didn't see it as good science fiction.
GR: Any idea why?
PKD: No. I have no theory. It's enigmatic to me. I don't understand it.
GR: In terms of chronology, **Martian Time-Slip** was before these other novels? (Judging from its 1963 serialization it preceded almost everything in this period after **High Castle** and probably **Game Players**).
PKD: I think it probably was. I think so. I went on a binge. I found something that was a compromise between what I wanted to write and what the market would buy. In other words it was not exactly what I wanted to write, and it was marketable, and it had enough of what I wanted to do in it to make it worth my interest. But if you'll notice most of those books were printed by minor publishers -- Ace, you know, and some real weird little publishers. They weren't hard cover. I didn't sell another hardcover book (after **High Castle**) until I sold **Three Stigmata** (in 1965) to Larry Ashmead at Doubleday. Remember I'd sold **Time Out of Joint** to Lippicott, and then I'd sold **Man in the High Castle** to Putnam, and then I was back selling to the goddamn paperbacks again, selling to Ace again. I was back right where I'd been. And the only thing I could was Ace, was then in a position to sell anything I wrote for them.

That was reasonably conventional. They could buy from me one novel after another and bring out four in one year. By then Ace was very successful and my stuff was selling pretty well. I could have written a hundred and sold a hundred to Ace. And I had terrible economic pressures on me at that time...I developed several ulcers and had to be hospitalized in this period.
GR: But I do find these books of very high quality.

PKD: Yeah, well by that point I had found my own kind of writing. I was doing my own type of writing. I was not a conventional writer, I was not a derivation of Alfred Bester or A.E. van Vogt. I was writing something that had really no precedent in the field. I was drawing on the Japanese novel, I was drawing on the French novel, I had really created a new kind of novel was what I had really done. I had really created an idiosyncratic novel that nobody else in the world was doing. Except maybe some of the Japanese who were writing. And nobody was reading them and so the American public I was unique.

I was very happy doing that kind of novel. They all had the same elements of humor -- they were balanced, they were beautifully balanced between humor and tragedy. I think. I wouldn't say I had a formula, but I would say I had a structure which I resorted to over and over again. It was my own. I had found my own idiom, and I was happy in it, and I was being paid for it, but I had suffered a great defeat with **Martian Time-Slip.** If I had sold that, say, to Viking or Harper and Row, or Scribner's, then I would have gone on to a much higher quality, more literate, more profound kind of novel. And this is something that I tend to forget and I don't tend to talk about very much. I finally had forgotten that there had been that defeat with **Martian Time-Slip.** There would have been following **Martian Time-Slip** a much higher kind, a much better novel. Which now we'll never know what it would have consisted of. Because I never went on. It would have been **Man in the High Castle, Martian Time-Slip,** and then X, and I can't even project now what that would have been. When it went so completely, it's too late now to retrieve it.

GR: What you did was good, so --

PKD: Well I did have to compromise, and I had thought that I could do anything I wanted after **Man in the High Castle.** Remember, only a few Hugo Awards had been given out at

that point. It was not an old institution. There had been four preceding mine. The prestige was enormous. Just incredible.
GR: Next came **The Three Stigmata of Palmer Eldritch** (1965).
PKD: Well now that might be what I would have gone on to do. I deduce now from internal evidence that that would be the kind of thing I wanted a lot of, where I was getting into themes of great metaphysical profundity. I was becoming very interested in religion and metaphysics.

That was written in connection with my becoming an adult convert to the Episcopal Church, and my becoming involved in Christianity, and my sense of the reality of the diabolical, whichis a carry-over from my prior interest in Zoroaster. For me Evil was as real a force as Good. There was God and there was the Anti-God. It was really a study of Deity as Evil and Good as Human. The good side was human and the evil side was deity. It's like man being confronted with a murderous God. It's essentially a diabolical novel.

Somebody called it a Satanic bible once. And in a way that's true. Because the Eucharist is not parodied, it's metamorphisized into a diabolical Eucharist. But I was developing a fairly profound idea of the Eucharist at that point. I had never been in a sacrodotal church before, and I was beginning to get a really profound idea of what the Eucharist was all about. But I had a sense of the evil of the world, a kind of Manichean sense, and so I tended to view these things as diabolical.

I was really being confronted by the problem of Absolute Evil, which I had dealth with somewhat in **Man in the High Castle.** But in **The Three Stigmata** the sense of Absolute Evil really comes out. It wasn't just a question of explaining suffering -- it wasn't as simple as that. it was a question of explaining just what I felt was the absolute evil in the world.

And I think this goes back to the study of the Nazis. As you trace it through the **Man in the High Castle** you can see it. The research I did on the Nazis was for **Man in the High Castle**, and then I became interested in theology and metaphysics, and all of a sudden the idea of a transcendental evil is coming out.

* * * * *

CHAPTER 23

The Novels of the Early Sixties:

The Simulacra / Clans of the Alphane Moon / The Zap Gun and The Penultimate Truth

"It Would Make a Great Film" / Dr. Bloodmoney

The Many Versions of The Unteleported Man

4-22-81

GR: In your early Sixties books, you get these incredible, multi-layered, multi-character plots. I wanted to ask you specifically about **The Simulacra,** which I think is the ultimate extension of your fragmentation (of narrative, in the Second Period).

PKD: Yeah, it is. Definitely. I once diagrammed it, after I'd

written it, sold it, and it had been published. One day I sat down, read it over, and drew a diagram, just to see if by any chance it all cohered. It doesn't. It can't be made to work out. There are people who just don't have any relationship with some of the other people in that group.
GR: Well, that's not necessary. There's these three record company people who fly up to Oregon at the beginning of the novel, and for most of the novel they sit in the jungle there, after they've met the pianist's wife. That's all. And they meet the chuppers at the end. That's all they're needed for.
PKD: There's a lot of book there for 75¢. Or 60¢, whatever. There's a lot of book for that amount of money.

My idea is to put as much into the book as I can put in. In other words I want to give the reader as much as I can give him.

9-30-81

GR: Clans of the Alphane Moon (1964)?
PKD: Well that was my interest in psychiatry. I was beginning to read a lot of books on psychiatry. I'd always been fascinated by abnormal mental states. It fits in with my interest in plural realities, like the Joan Reiss section of **Eye in the Sky** where a strange reality is perceived by the psychotic person. The psychotic is one whose experience of reality is radically different than ours. And this is something that fascinates me. It absolutely still fascinates me. But now I'd rather simply avoid it. I find it more repellent than anything else. The world of the psychotic is no longer of any interest to me. I want to put as much distance between me and the psychotic person as I can put. I suffered too much at the hands of psychotic people to want to be around them any more. They do not intrigue me any longer. When I see schizophrenia I just walk away.

4-22-81

...**(Clans of the Alphane Moon)** was a labor of love. The story of the survival value of various forms of psychosis. Did they have any utilitarian utility? It seemed to me in many ways they did. If not in our culture, in other cultures perhaps. (The clans of the book are made up of paranoids, schizophrenics, manic-depressives, and etc. who can band together when necessary to defend their colony). I liked that book. I enjoyed it very much.

GR: So did I. It's very underrated. Do you have books that you consider pot-boilers?

PKD: Oh, a lot of them are pot-boilers. Well, they weren't intentionally, they worked out that way. I always write it as well as I can. But sometimes I just don't have the sacred fire to enflame my talent into, you know, a level of genius and what I wind up with is some turkey like **Zap Gun**.

GR: You think **Zap Gun**'s a turkey?

PKD: Well, the first half is totally unreadable, I don't know where or what --

GR: Well the first three chapters are hard to get into.

PKD: I can hardly reconstruct the thinking that underlay the first half of that book. Just totally unintelligible.

GR; I thought it was a self-parody. Your early '60s books are full of this Cold War satire, and social criticim, and **Zap Gun** takes off from that into extreme variations. It builds nicely, and the ending is good.

PKD: There are a couple of good things in it. But at that point I was beginning to run out on that phase of my writing. There was no point in pursuing that kind of novel any further. I mean **Zap Gun** proved it. I was really recycling, in unintentional self-parody. It was not intentional self-parody, but it amounted to it.

I was trying to write a serious book, but by that time --

GR: You have things like "the Garbage Can Banger" (as a deadly weapon in the Cold War defense build-up) and so

forth, that are comic variations on things like "the Stink of Shrink" (the made up plagues used to terrorize the populace) in **Penultimate Truth.**
PKD: Those were written simultaneously. I wrote them together, both under contract.
GR: What do you think of **Penultimate Truth?**
PKD: I don't know. It's certainly not a major book but it has a couple of good ideas in it. The idea of faking those skulls and sending them back in time (one of the book's sub-plots) or whatever the hell they did is ingenious as a way of setting somebody up.
GR: I thought that was fantastic. Any other novelist would have built a whole novel around that idea, and you just toss it off as a plot device.

If I were going to try and make a film out of any of your books, I'd pick that one.
PKD: That's the book the guys who sent me this coffee (an excellent brew we were drinking) want to make a film of. The guy involved is (Vernon) Zimmerman, who did **Fade to Black** (1980). Zimmerman called me. He's real nice. They want to do **Penultimate Truth.**
GR: I think it's an important book to do -- it's as true now as it was then, the way the government manipulates the Cold War to keep people in line. Have you seen their screenplay?
PKD: I haven't heard from them in a long time. I get their coffee, but I don't get word from them. I don't think they're going to pursue it. They have no money.
GR: If I were doing the script, I'd keep it from the viewpoint of the ant-tanker, Nicholas St. James, until half-way through, when he crawls up from underground into what he expects to be a radioactive wilderness, and instead it's all green and beautiful. Pow! Then he realizes they've all been faking, the "war" is just for power.
PKD: I think it would make a great film.

* * * * *

9-30-81

GR: The Zap Gun (1967, originally serialized in **Worlds of Tomorrow** in 1965-66 as "Project Plowshare").
PKD: That's been called -- (it's been) called a deliberate self-parody, but it wasn't. That was an attempt to write a serious novel. I was just under a great deal of stress at that time, I'd separated from my wife and was living back with my mother and step-father, and I was under contract to do two books at once, **The Penultimate Truth** and **Zap Gun,** and I did them both at once. In six weeks I did 1,200 pages. They are just not good books because I was writing much too fast, and I didn't have any real audience. The first 150 pages of **Zap Gun** I find actually unreadable. I can't read them. The last part is okay. The first part is just dreadful.
GR: Dr. Bloodmoney (1965).
PKD: That is an excellent book. I had been living in West Marin, in a rural community there (Point Reyes Station) for long enough to become familiar with it. I juxtaposed it with the Berkeley community which I had been a part of so the two of them are fused together into a post-Holocaust world that is really unique. It's a really unique world that I built up. It's not like any apocalyptic novel ever written. That's not what you'd expect to find after a Holocaust. So that's a very original book, I think. As a society, that's a very original society. And I'm impressed with that book. It's really definitely a unique book. In fiction, not just in science fiction, in fiction itself.

I was drawing on two very disparate communities, Berkeley and West Marin.
GR: It seems like an outgrowth in some ways of **Confessions of A Crap Artist** (set in West Marin).
PKD: Yes, it is.

* * * * *

GR: What about **The Unteleported Man?**

PKD: That was just written as a novelette for **Amazing** (actually published in **Fantastic, Amazing's** sister magazine, December 1964). That was just a way to make money. They offered me double their normal word rate if I'd do a novelette based on the cover. They had a cover drawn. And I did that. It wasn't very good.

4-22-81

GR: I heard that half of it was suppressed, or deleted, by the publisher (in its book form publication, 1966).
PKD: No,. The original version is as I wrote it, but when Wollheim bought it he wanted to add another 50% more, and I wrote another 50% more, but he didn't like it. It was too spacey for him, too much acid stuff.

So he never published the second half, and Berkley wants to bring it out, but it requires revision. The two parts don't fit together at all. The second part is much better than the part that's been published. It's quite imaginative and quite radical. I mean, quite experimental....But I can't get into that space of **The Unteleported Man** to rewrite it (to tie together the two halves). I can't get back into the action-adventure stuff, so it's hung fire for several years.
GR: What happens in the second half?
PKD: I forget. I haven't looked at it for years.

That part is very good. It's real weird. I don't know where my head was at in those days. I'd just left Anne. I was living in Oakland.

* * * * *

I just have an awful time going back to that action stuff, **The Unteleported Man** type of thing. It's very painful, excruciating.
GR: Wouldn't it just be a matter of cleaning up the discrepancies?

PKD: I just can't turn back. It's impossible to turn back. It's just incredible.

I know this sounds silly, but that's one reason why I didn't do this novelization to the **Blade Runner** thing (see Chapter 32). I think part of it is that I have a terrible fear that I'll abreact back to that, and not be able to get out of it. It took me years.

(After Phil's death Berkley Books brought out the "complete" **Unteleported Man,** complete or rather incomplete with the previously "supressed" second half -- which was missing a few pages. These were left as gaps in the 1983 reissue.

(However, after publication of this version, a new first chapter written by Dick in 1979 was discovered, together with some other revisions that together with two "fill-in" pages written by John Sladek to cover the remaining gaps in the manuscript was scheduled for publication by Gollancz in Britain in May 1984. This version, as definitive as we are likely to get - unless of course new material by Dick turns up - has been titled **Lies, Inc.**)

* * * * *

CHAPTER 24
Hiatus / Writer's Block
Now Wait for Last Year and The Crack in Space
A Collaboration

4-22-81

GR: You say you have this year long gap in your writing after you left Anne?
PKD: Yes.
GR: Counter-Clock World was the first one in this new phase?
PKD: Yes.

GR: I have to think about this, 'cause this might break up my whole period thing.
PKD: No, it fits exactly. Exactly. (It's) absolutely correct.
GR: You go from the multi-character plots of the early '60s, to the Third Period plots centering around two to four people.
PKD: I wanted to develop the characters more.

9-30-81

GR: And so we move into the late '60s.
PKD: Now this really is a different period of writing than the one we've been talking about (the early '60s), when we started talking about this group, starting with **Counter-Clock World** (1967). My marriage to Anne broke up, I'd left Marin County, I'd gone to live in Oakland, met Nancy, and gone back to Marin County, but to another part, to the urban part (San Rafael). I had a different marriage, a different child, different house, different community, and was writing less and having more trouble.

For the first time I was beginning to have trouble writing, I was beginning to show some writer's block. After I left Anne in '64 I had almost a year of intense writer's block. Partly it was due to fatigue, partly it was due to having written so much. I'm not sure it was true writer's block, but it might not have been just fatigue.

I began writing in great difficulty. I took much more time with each book. I didn't just bat 'em right out. For one thing I knew I was writing for a hardcover market. I was writing for Doubleday at that point. I was striving to write a better book.

Now Wait for Last Year (1966) I think is a very, very well written novel. I really love it a lot. And **Do Androids Dream of Electric Sheep?** (1968) likewise.

But my productivity had fallen off a lot. I was beginning

to really wear out. The first signs of overwork were really beginning to show up in my life. I was getting really tired.
GR: Counter-Clock World was the first one you wrote (in this period), but not the first one you published?
PKD; Right. The first one I wrote after I left Anne, and after my hiatus. It was a short hiatus by my later hiatuses, but I was unable to write for awhile. I did that second half of **The Unteleported Man,** and Wollheim wouldn't buy it -- and I was messed up, my marriage had broken up...
GR: In my essay on you, I identified a break in here, the beginning of a dinstinctly different period.
PKD: Yes, and you identified that exactly right. Chronologically you got it perfectly. And that was very astute of you, because every single person who has analyzed my writing has failed to see that there was a clear demarcation.
GR: How about **The Crack in Space** (1966)?
PKD: Oh, that didn't work out. It was a terrible novel. That was written while I was still married to Anne. ("Cantata 140," published as a novella in 1964, comprises the first half of that book).
GR: So it's really carry-over from the Second Period.
PKD: Ace had bought so many it took years to bring them out.
GR: And **The Ganymede Takeover** (co-authored by Ray Nelson, 1967)?
PKD: The Ganymede Takeover was written before **Counter-Clock World** too. And sold to Ace and backlogged. That was just an attempt to break my writer's block by collaborating with a friend. I couldn't write. He wrote the book and I just spruced it up for sale. I can't understand under the circumstances how I was even able to do that. I was suffering terribly from the loss of the girls (his daughter and Anne's two daughters), living in the slums of Oakland, with no money. It was my first contact with street people. I was running into street people for the first time in my life,

and not handling that well at all. And I was really going down hill fast. I was definitely having problems with my inter-personal world. My life was not working out too well.

* * * * *

CHAPTER 25
Ray Nelson / Writing The Ganymede Takeover (Interview with Ray Nelson)

10-12-81

PKD: I met (Ray Nelson) in '64 when I was in the Bay Area. I liked him a lot and we did that joke novel **The Ganymede Takeover** just for laughs. He'd write part and I'd write part - we had a lot of fun doing that, it was something to do. He'd mail me his part, and he'd include pictures of beetles. All these pictures of beetles, it was like bubble gum cards, would fall out. (laughing) It was really, really great. He has a great sense of humor.

One time this friend of ours got arrested and thrown in jail, and we bailed him out. We put up the bail money. (chuckling) What the guy did then was he stole somebody's car and left the state. Ray had put up part of the money and I had put up part of the money and the guy put up part of the money. Instead of phoning me up - we were living in the East Bay and it wasn't a toll call - Ray sent me a postcard, he said "X has stolen -----'s car and has left California. Yours in the Bowels of Christ, Ray Nelson." (laughing)

The guy came back. He burned up the car and came back to California, so we didn't have to come up with the 350 bucks.

(Ray Faraday Nelson, co-author of **The Ganymede Takeover,** had this to say when I interviewed him in June, 1982 about the creation of that work):

RFN: Carol Carr and Terry Carr were part of his circle. Marion Zimmer Bradley, J.G. Newkom and J.G. Newkom's then-wife, and Poul Anderson and Karen Anderson were part of the circle. (And myself and Phil, and Avram Davidson and Grania Davidson).

When I think of the circle I think of afternoons at Phil's place in Oakland, where we would gather around the dining room table, and throw ideas out at each other, and improvise communal stories. A lot of ideas that have become embodied in the work of various members of that circllce (came from there). The first ideas for Marion

circle (came from there). The first ideas for Marion Bradley's Darkover series were hatched out in those plotted sessions. One of which -- I think the idea for **The Bloody Sun** (1964) I remember - was held at her place, with the same personnel present.

There was no one to check one's credentials as one came in. Anyone who came and sat down at this table were part of the plotting session. That book that Phil and I did together, **The Ganymede Takeover**, was the result of one of these plotting sessions. Some of the ideas in there are from

Davidson and some are from Poul Anderson and some are from Karen Anderson. As well as Phil and I. And J.G. Newkom contributed some ideas too. He's never become a professional writer, but he was nevertheless a contributing member of these brainstorming sessions.

The book grew out of those afternoons when the circle sat around and threw ideas into a hat. On that day Phil and I threw in more ideas than the others did, and I took the ideas home and wrote an outline based on the ideas - stringing them all together into a logical and coherent form - and then Phil took that outline and wrote it over again.

The starting point was a story Phil had written called "The Little Black Box" (1964), which had already been published. He was looking for ways to expand that story, and that was the problem that he set for us as we had that brainstorming session. The story, which then was called "The Earth's Diurnal Course," and later was retitled **The Ganymede Takeover** by Scott Meredith, then was born out of that second outline that Phil wrote based on my outline.

I wrote the first chapter, and Phil wrote a very detailed outline, and we sent it to Scott Meredith, and Scott thought it would never sell, but he routinely put it out to market anyway. And it really didn't sell for a long time. But then Ace picked it up. And by that time Phil had already sold a portion of it - of the part that was already written - elsewhere, and so we had to rewrite that section.

We began -- we wrote the whole book before we knew it was sold, as sort of a fun exercise. Phil would write a chapter and send it to me, and I would write a chapter and send it to him, and then we would rewrite each other's chapters, and then we would meet at intervals. Along with the chapters we were sending back and forth we would send all sorts of miscellaneous odds and ends, like Beatle posters, and bubble gum cards, and pictures of cats. Phil and I were both cat fiends. I have 12 cats, just to show you how far it goes.

So we were really just having a wonderful time with the

book. Didn't really care whether it sold or not. And we finished the book before it was sold. When Phil thought that it was not going to be able to be sold in its complete version, he took a part of it and sold it separately. And then some kind of copyright problem made it so I had to write a new section to fill up that hole. There was a period in between the times that the book was written in its first form, and when it was written in its second form, that this hole (needed to be) filled up, and during that time I had forgotten that a fellow named Gus Swenesgard was in the book married. So in the first part of the book he's married. In the second part of that book, he's single. And there's no explanation for that. Kirsten (Nelson) spotted it immediately. Almost no one else has spotted it.

GR: What about the Joan Hiashi charcter?

RFN: She's a combination of Nancy (Dick) and Kirsten. The vision scene part is Nancy, and the adventurous part, the career girl part, is Kirsten...We blended this visionary character with Kirsten's intense realism and drive, and came up with a character we thought was a balance of the two of them. The book is dedicated to the two of them, for that reason. The chief character is half of one and half of the other.

GR: Did Phil often use actual people as characters?

RFN: I think he did, but I can only trace a few...Kirsten and myself appear in **Do Androids Dream of Electric Sheep?** as two of the androids, and also Kirsten appears as two different characters in **Flow My Tears.** She's Christine and somebody else with a similar name. Two different aspects of her character being portrayed.

(In **Androids**) he describes me as having an air of spurious authority.

GR: There's this family of androids hiding out in this decaying building.

RFN: That's right....He used actual incidents, too, slightly embroidered. There's an incident, I guess it's in **Flow My Tears,** about a rabbit whose tail is bitten by a dog, and how the rabbit turns around and faces the dog. That's based on an actual rabbit, that was my rabbit, and the dog belonged to "Joe Chup" (false name) who was a realistic novelist. He had this fierce wolfdog he had with him at all times, and that wolfdog tried to attack my rabbit, but my rabbit stood that wolfdog off after the dog bit his tail.

And Phil, with his usual antic humor, portrayed "Joe" - who was really a macho type, a former featherweight boxing champion he says - as an aunt in that book. Aunt Fanny or some such thing.

That's characteristic of the funny turns that these characterizations take. There's always a little satirical bite to these real life characters --they're caricatures rather than characterizations. "Joe" was really mad about it too. He said, I ought to sue him; if I could prove that was me, I'd sue him...

The Ganymede Takeover started when he was living in Oakland, and was finished when he was living in San Rafael (with Nancy).

GR: That would be in 1965, and it came out '67. What section of it did you rewrite?

RFN: There is a part in there about Mercer that's changed.

GR: Mercer's from "The Little Black Box." (The Christ-like preacher with his religion of empathy). He's in **Do Androids Dream.**

RFN: That's right, but originally that black box part (through which Mercer communicates his pain to his disciples) was in **The Ganymede Takeover.** It isn't in there any more, see. It's the missing part. He used to say he plagiarized himself.

GR: Who typed the final draft?

RFN: The final draft was done by Phil. The final draft is cut down from a longer version by me. I wrote a final draft which was too long, and he quite radically cut that to meet Ace's word count limitations. Especially the ending, there's a sequence where a character is walking up a hill, that contained a lot of flashback material, a lot of experimental writing by me. That hit the cutting room floor. And there's more stuff about model planes (one of the "worm kings of Ganymede" is an avid collector), and some incidental humorous material that had to go.

So Phil's final version was more like a radical editing of my final version. It didn't contain any new material.

GR: Do you have the original long draft?

RFN: No.

(Ray Nelson credited Phil with the talking taxi in the book, but said he was drawing on his own life in the creation of the black militant Percy X - in his youth he was an organizer for CORE - and the southern cracker, Gus Swenesgard. He grew up in the South as an outsider and had reason to fear the type. However--)

GR: What is your attitude toward aliens? Usually the extraterrestrials in Phil's books are friendly, but here the Ganymedians are as a group hostile.

RFN: I think that the characteristics of those creatures were set by Poul Anderson. That is Poul Anderson's contribution to the pot. He's the one who outlined the basic nature of those aliens. Poul Anderson's stories generally have a higher level of violence, and a less sympathetic attitude towards aliens, than either Phil or me...

GR: What is your attitude towards the isolation of individuals as opposed to their joining together in some sort of group mind? The book takes an ambivilent position, it seems to me.

RFN: Ah, yes. Well that is a reflection of something Phil and I have talked about a lot. I am an organizer. I am one of the people who helped organize CORE (The Congress of Racial Equality). And a lot of other things, too many to mention. So I'm a collectivist, of sorts. And Phil is an individualist.

That ambivilence (in the book) reflects many long, philosophical discussions involving chiefly Kirsten, myself, and Phil. Because Kirsten and Phil agree on that. They are both strong individualists.

Phil and I were satirizing each other's position. Phil was satirizing my position, in the group mind (of Ganymede). I was satirizing his position in the isolation tank (sequence).
GR: The isolation tank was new then, wasn't it?
RFN: It was only a theoretical idea. Now it's a reality -- a popular reality.
GR: It hasn't had the same effect (as in the book -- where it is used to destroy personalities).
RFN: It was only an idea -- nobody knew what would happen whem somebody used the tank.
GR: The Dr. Balkani character (the Earth's "Chief of the Bureau of Psychedelic Research") --
RFN: That's my character. I invented him.
GR: What attitude did you have toward psychiatry?
RFN: (Ironically) A hostile one.
GR: (Laughing) Why?
RFN: Because I don't really think they understand the human mind. I think that they say they know a lot of things, and they don't. I'd rather say I don't know, than to say the kind of things that they think they know.

I think Phil agrees with that. There is **something** going on in the world, which Jung called synchronicity, and that sometimes is interpreted in a religious way. There's a connectedness of things, and there's a kind of coincidence that goes beyond coincidence, which psychiatry doesn't take into account.

There's one way that more books by Phil might surface, and that is that some people - including myself - have outlines that date from that Oakland period. I have two outlines for prospective novels, which if they were published would have to be published as co-authored, as the plot is co-authored. The actual writing of the book would be done by me. I think Poul Anderson has at least one also.

So there might be still some more collaborations forthcoming, in the same way there were (posthumous) collaborations with Robert E. Howard. People took up his plot outlines and wrote new "Conan" material.

There are two books that I have that I know about. One of them is called "The Swastika and the Cross," and it's a sequel to **Man in the High Castle.** The other one is called "The Whale Mouth Colony," and it's a sequel to another one of Phil's books. The title escapes me.

("The Whale Mouth Colony" project was undoubtedly an attempt to take up and use the unpublished second half of **The Unteleported Man,** which was finally reunited with its parent in 1983. Most of the second half of **The Unteleported Man** takes place in the "Whale Mouth Colony" 18 light years from Earth where the hero of the novel has in fact been teleported to).

* * * * *

CHAPTER 26

The Novels of the Late Sixties:

Counter-Clock World "I Was Very Happy" Do Androids Dream of Electric Sheep? and Ubik "Ossification:" A Maze of Death and Our Friends From Frolix 8 / The Ubik Screenplay / Galactic Pot-Healer / We Can Build You

9-30-81

GR: Which brings us to **Counter-Clock World** (1967), my favorite of all your novels.
PKD: That was the first novel I wrote after I met Nancy, and Nancy is a very beautiful and tender and loving and a very sweet person, she infused in my writing a different feeling for peole than I'd ever had before. Her

sister, too, is a very, very beautiful loving and tender person. I was very fond of her sister, and her both. It entered beauty and tenderness into my life and changed my whole attitude towards people and towards life. I was very happy at that time.

But I was afraid that that marriage would not last, as I had had three broken marriages prior to it. And as I foresaw it didn't last. (The couple separated in 1970).

GR: But if you were so happy writing **Counter-Clock World** -- that is a very tragic novel.

PKD: Yeah, because I saw that on the way. I foresaw the loss of these women. I'm very good at foreseeing things. I have a tremendous ability to foresee things.

GR: Well I hope you're foreseeing something good now. **Divine Invasion** is so up.

PKD: So is the Bishop Archer novel. Tremendous positive ending. Just incredible. In fact my agent said he'd never encountered anything like it outside of the Gospel. For sudden reversal, complete reversal. Like the scene at the tomb. And he's not Christian, he's Jewish. He said only in the Gospel do you find the sudden inbreaking of the sublime and the beautiful, when it looks as if everything's lost.

GR: Do Androids Dream of Electric Sheep? (1968)

PKD: That was written when things were really quite stable for me. Nancy and I had a house and a child and a fair amount of money. Things were good.

At that point I was contrasting Nancy's warmth with the coldness of the people I'd known before. I was beginning to develop the idea of the human versus the android, the bipedal humanoid that is not essentially human. She had shown me for the first time what a real human being could be like, tender and loving and vulnerable. And I was beginning to contrast that to what I had been brought up with.

GR: Ubik (1969).
PKD: Ubik started off conventionally, and then all of a sudden I realized I was writing too conventional a novel, and I panicked and just decided to go for broke on anything I could think of, and lucked out. I lucked out because I'd been reading the Tibetian Book of the Dead and I'd had some interesting theological ideas. So I had the material to put in. But that was a rather desperate effort to infuse something original into that book, whereas the original concept was not original.

I was still writing for Larry Ashmead (at Doubleday), and he liked **Ubik** a lot. It was a favorite of his, of all those that I sold him. But I had to pull that out of the fire.

Now there is an element of desperation that began to show up in the writing, a recognition that I'm beginning to repeat myself and an attempt to do something new when I wrote that one. What we're seeing with that, though, is the beginning of an ossification in my writing where I **am** beginning to repeat myself. There was beginning to be evidence that my whole format had frozen, and I wasn't advancing. **Ubik** was a desperate attempt to advance it.

And then of course that's followed by **A Maze of Death** (1970). And **A Maze of Death** is really a desperate attempt to come up with something new. In no way is it new. It repeats familiar things with a multi-foci basis and the epistemological theme, the reality versus irreality. That's the last gasp of those things that had become my stock in trade. At that point I could not go on. I had exhausted all the possibilities in the type of thing I had been doing.

So with **Maze of Death** there was no way there could be a further novel based on those things. Something new had to be done. And the next novel, well, the next novel was **Our Friends from Frolix 8** (1970). And that is a throwaway novel. That was simply written for money. It was not intended to be anything else but a novel for Ace Books. It

was under contract for Ace Books. It was simply a regression. Much like **Vulcan's Hammer.** It's an equivalent to **Vulcan's Hammer.**
GR: But it's so much better than **Vulcan's Hammer.**
PKD: At that point I was beginning to become desperate because I was petrified, I mean ossified in my field. My structure, my characters were ossified. Everything.

4-22-81

GR: Our Friends from Frolix 8 is a reworking of themes from **The Unteleported Man** --
PKD: Yeah, I was commissioned to do that by Ace Books for the money. I was very short on money. I reverted back when I wrote **Frolix 8.**
GR: I think it's very good. Very serious, too. You have the question of whether or not to trust the alien.
PKD: Yeah.
GR: And the likable evil dictator, sort of a cross between Stanton Brose (**The Penultimate Truth**) and Arnie Kott (**Martian Time-Slip**).
PKD: What was it, Sandra Miesel talked about my "modular building blocks" (out of which Phil built his novels).

* * * * *

GR: You wrote a screenplay for **Ubik,** didn't you?
PKD: Yes I did. It's the only screenplay I've ever written. They weren't able to get the finance for it. They bought the screenplay -- that was Jean-Pierre Gorin. He had worked with (Jean-luc) Godard, you know (in France, in the 1969-72 period, and afterwards alone in America, which would date the **Ubik** screenplay in the 1973 period or later). He was hoping for (Francis Ford) Coppola to back it, but couldn't get the money.

Then Jean-Pierre got sick with liver trouble, and was in the hospital. He may be dead.
GR: When did he get sick? I saw him in November (1980, at the San Francisco Film Festival).
PKD: (delighted) Oh! Thank God, he's not dead.
GR: He's very healthy. He showed his new film (**Poto and Cabengo**), about these twins in San Diego with an invented language.
PKD: Oh, thank God he's all right!

(The Dick **Ubik** screenplay exists, and is very interesting, both for its very original grappling with the language of cinema, and for its rethinking of **Ubik.** The screenplay's ending, particularly, is very beautiful and mysterious -- better, even, than the book's).

* * * * *

9-30-81

GR: Did you write **Galactic Pot Healer** (1969) after **Ubik**? Because we now have **Ubik - Maze of Death - Frolix.**
PKD: I think it was after **Ubik.** Somewhere I just dashed off **Galactic Pot Healer,** and there I just winged it. I had no plot or anything. It was very much like that second half of **The Unteleported Man,** just sheer -- it's almost like I was faking it. Just trying to dazzle with a pyrotechnic display. Some people liked it and some people didn't. Ursula LeGuin liked it, and John Brunner knew that it was out of control. He told me, look, that book got out of your control. And he was quite right. I had no idea from page to page what I was doing to do. On the other hand that's true of a lot of my other writing that I didn't know what I was going to do. It's just that **Galactic Pot Healer** begins to show that there's just no preconception on my part at all.

4-22-81

GR: We Can Build You came out as a book in 1972, but was first published in magazine form (in 1969-70) as "A. Lincoln, Simulacrum." Was it written in '69?
PKD: No, that was a long time earlier. That's an early book. I don't even know when I wrote it. I honestly do not know. The manuscript sat around in the closet for a long time. Ted White knew about it and asked to buy it for **Amazing.** I believe, from internal evidence, that it was written in the '50s.
GR: It would seem to fit in with the Third Period (late '60s) novels, because of the cold young female character (Pris, the schizoid, who seems linked with similar characters in **Do Androids Dream, Our Friends from Frolix 8,** etc.) and also the sadness of the two men in love with the same woman (the central male the older one, as in **Counter-Clock World**) -- it fits in with the sadness of the late '60s books.
PKD: But, see, that essentially was not designed by me as science fiction. That was one of my hybrid books. I had an idea which did not work out. Talk about noble ideas -- this is really a noble idea. That was a book that would bridge science fiction and mainstream. And that was supposed to be one of them. Where there'd be science fiction elements but there'd also be elements of a mainstream book.

And that was the main one. It would be a continuum from **The World Jones Made** to **We Can Build You** to **Confessions of a Crap Artist**, would form a continuum, an unbroken continuum, where there's no sharp delineation between the three. And so I was trying to make a continuum out of my two parallel streams of writing, my science fiction and my mainstream, by writing something that would bridge both. And I could never do it.

Another one was **Martian Time-Slip.** That was actually a projection on my part of a kind of hybrid thing, where I used real human characters, but in a science fictional background. And that was not well received at the time.

* * * * *

CHAPTER 27

The Early Seventies: Hiatus / Flow My Tears, The Policeman Said

"Writing Autobiographically" / Deus Irae and Roger Zelazny

9-30-81

GR: After **Our Friends from Frolix 8** in 1970, nothing original comes out till **Flow My Tears, the Policeman Said,** in 1974.

PKD: **Flow My Tears** was written in '70. I wrote that in what was the worst period of my life. I hope it was the worst period of my life. I hope I don't ever have to go through anything like that again. Nancy had left me while I was working on the book, and I finished the book, even though she had taken our daughter and left. I was sitting there in a four-bedroom, two bathroom house by myself trying to finish the book. The theme of the book became autobiographical because I was suffering so much from the loss of her that I have the Police General's sister die, and then the tremendous grief and loneliness that he feels, and that was really all based on losing Nancy. (The break-up of this marriage was quite necessary from her point of view. See my interview with Nancy Hackett in the third book of this series).

So at that point I am writing autobiographically because I cannot keep out the autobiographical elements. It isn't like **Crap Artist. Crap Artist** is autobiographical. But that's because I decided to write an autobiographical novel. In this case I could not sit there and write that book, with what was happening to me in my actual life excluded. What was happening to me in my actual life forced its way into the book, and dominated the book. And I wrote version after version of the ending of that book, rewrote it and rewrote it, in order to get down on paper the feelings I was feeling about Nancy leaving me, because I had really loved her. I think she was probably the most wonderful person I had ever known. I wanted to get down how it felt to lose someone you loved that much. So I just kept refining and refining the ending, and then when it came time to type up the final draft to send it off I was too tired. I had done about six versions of the book before I was satisfied. I just put the manuscript away and didn't pick it up again until 1973, when I was down here in Orange County.

I had gone to Canada, and to Orange County. The manuscript was in my lawyer's safe and I had him mail it down and I did the final draft. We went through eleven versions in all. Eleven different drafts.

GR: Was the book influenced at all by anything that happened between 1970 and 1973?

PKD: No, because the book was written. There were some stylistic touches that I put in. A few things about my aversion to drugs, as I had developed a strong aversion to drugs. But the book was essentially written. In fact I found I'd even begun to type up the final draft, the first maybe hundred pages were already typed up. I didn't even remember doing it. I actually started tying the final version and then giving up. I was too tired to do it.

GR: Well now, I'll have to completely rewrite my theories (about **Flow** marking the beginning of a new period for Phil, rather than the end of an old one). They say in science that a theory is only good until it runs into a fact.

PKD: Well, let's hope that's true of the rest of life. Not just in science.

GR: Then we have **Deus Irae** (co-authored by Roger Zelazny, 1976).

PKD: Well I'd started that in '64, and then been unable to complete it simply because I didn't know enough about Christianity. And I brought in Roger Zelazny, who is far more educated and intelligent than I am, and we just worked on it on and off throughout the years. We kind of kept it on the back burner. Roger would do a little bit and send it to me, and I'd do a little bit and send it back to him. And we never really thought we'd finish it. Then all of a sudden the day came -- Roger did such a long stretch that there was little if anything left for me to do. I just did the ending and I sent it off.

So it was kind of like just an amateur thing that we were doing just for the pleasure of it. Roger told me he'd read parts to people, and we enjoyed the parts, but we never really thought we'd finish the book. It was kind of just something to do. We were very good friends and it was a lot of fun to keep doing that. It was almost like sending a letter back and forth.

* * * * *

10-12-81

GR: You're good friends with Zelazny?
PKD: Yeah, we're real good friends. I really love Roger. He is the greatest guy in the universe. I had read his works, stories and novels, **Lord of Light** (1967) the novel -- and just thought that he was simply the greatest writer to come into the field after I came into the field, that is, who for me was a new writer. I got a chance in '68 to meet him and tell him so, and like to me it was -- I still remember being brought up to his hotel room, being introduced to him, and being able to tell him how much I liked his writing. We kept in touch, and I turned over the uncompleted manuscript of **Deus Irae** to him, and he finished it.
GR: Still see him?
PKD: I saw him in '77 when I was in France. And he was the same as ever, really great. Oh, and I saw him recently, dammit, I saw him earlier this year. He was doing an autograph party at a science fiction store here in Orange County. We talked and we all had dinner, and he told a real funny story about a cat. I've told this story and they all think it's morbid. I thought it was the funniest story I had ever heard. Maybe it was the way he told it.

This person has this real indolent cat , that's incredibly fat, and so greedy and so lazy that it would sleep by its dish. And one time they went over to it, 'cause they noticed the food was uneaten, (and) the cat had been dead for two days. (laughing) I can just see this gigantic indolent cat just expiring from obesity right by its dish. It never does anything but go to its dish, so they don't notice it. They come back later and the food isn't eaten, so they deduce the cat is dead.

A real story, he said. Really happened.

* * * * *

CHAPTER 28
The Late Seventies:
A Scanner Darkly
The Drug Culture: "I Wrote That To Record Them" / Donna / VALIS

9-30-81

GR: A Scanner Darkly (1977) was your first book, then, to incorporate your experiences in the early 70's
PKD: That's correct. I had lived in the drug subculture after Nancy left in '70, and in '71, and the very first month of '72. But I left in February of '72 to go to Canada, and then I had come down to Orange County, and was no longer a part of

the drug subculture. I wanted to get down on paper the memory of those people that I had known in the drug subculture. I wrote that to record them. And also as an attack on drugs because I had seen it kill so many people that I now was dedicated to preaching the gospel of the dangers of drugs. I had seen too many people die.

* * * * *

4-22-81

GR: What can you say about **A Scanner Darkly** that doesn't come out in the afterword, which is so moving, or the book itself?
PKD: I think I got down those characters before they faded from my memory. That's the main thing.

I wrote it as soon as I could, after I left the dope culture. As soon as I could I started writing them down. I planned to do that as soon as I went to Canada -- we're talking about essentially a week after I left the dope culture I was already trying to write about those people.

The real question was, could I get those people down on paper before their speech cadences faded from my mind. And I really think I got them down. **Now** it would be impossible to get those people down. When I read **Scanner**, it's like those people come back to life for me.

I rejoice in the fact that I was able to get the time to get those guys down on paper. They're all gone.

Everybody says Donna is a bad person (The dealer/double-agent who sets up the protagonist, Bob Arctor). The girl it's based on - it's essentially a creative rendering of that girl - I had only admiration for. I never felt that her incredible duplicity was bad. She lived in a stratum of society, she lived in a milieu, where deceit was required in order to survive. In other words, without that quality of deceit she would be dead. She would be dead. She would be killed within a matter of hours.

This was a girl who was a dope dealer. She was a **drug**

dealer, and she was a police informant at the same time. She'd been busted I guess -- she never told me why she'd become a police informant. But apparently she'd been busted, and given the option of becoming an informant or going to jail. And so she became an informant. And the drug dealing had to be kept a secret, and the informing had to be kept a secret. So she was in a very difficult spot. She was only 18 years old at the time.

How else can you be if you're a drug dealer who's also working with the police inspector? She had three identities: she had a regular job, and she still lived with her parents. She had to conceal from everybody that she dealt dope. And also she was an addict, that's another thing, looking back, she was probably a heroin addict too, amongst everything else. I'll never know. Heroin addicts don't come up to you and say I'm a heroin addict. She was apparently into major theft, as well as the drug dealing, she was probably into major rip-offs, working with a rip-off gang, to raise money for her habit.

She led a very complicated life, and I don't see that under those circumstances how she could be up-front with anybody at any time. But I was very fond of her.

GR: Do you know what happened to her?

PKD: No. Her boyfriend came over one time and said you'll never see her again, you'll never even know where she went, she's planning on cutting all her ties with just everybody, and start a new life. And damned if she didn't do it. Just vanished.

I certainly hope she did. She was the best friend I ever had. In all my life, I never had a better friend, nor do I think anyone could have a better friend.

But I got it down on paper, before the memory left. And a lot of people I've met who have read it and who are in the drug culture have said that it was the only book they'd ever found that got these people down. They sit and talk forever about nothing. You can spin the tape ahead four hours and they're still talking about virtually the same subject. No progress at all. They don't make progress.

* * * * *

9-30-81

GR: VALIS (1981) followed **A Scanner Darkly** as your next novel.
PKD: VALIS follows. But there again you see another marriage broken up, my marriage to Tessa. I'd written **Scanner** while Tessa and I were married -- in fact, she gets half the royalties on **Scanner.**

Again I'd lost a wife and child. And again the autobiographical elements force their way into the book, just as in **Flow My Tears** they'd forced their way in. And here I recognized that there was no way those autobiographical elements could be kept out. It was hopeless even to try. So rather than trying to keep them out, I welcomed them in and wrote a deliberate autobiographical novel. So it's more like **Confessions of a Crap Artist,** where the autobiographical element is deliberately included rather than forcing its way.

I wrote, in fact, a conventional version of **VALIS** that I scratched, which was not nearly as autobiographica and

scratched, which was not nearly as autobiographical and (instead) deliberately chose to adopt almost a non-novel format, almost a combination journal of my life, an account of my life. I got the idea from my introduction to **The Golden Man** (1980 collection of short stories), where I wrote that account of my life, and the idea came that I could carry it on to the full novel. It was not until I'd done the introduction to **The Golden Man** that I saw that as the way to go with **VALIS.** So that really derives from the introduction to **The Golden Man.** I happened to write that because I owed Berkley a book and I'd been paid and didn't want to give the money back. So they compromised on a story collection, but on the basis that I would do an extensive introduction. And having done that, I saw --

That's one of the first non-fiction things I'd ever written was the introduction to **Golden Man.** I hadn't written that much non-fiction. I saw a novel built around that loose, discursive, colloquial style. A discursive plot, a loose structure, and a colloquial style. Vernacular style. About me and my friends. So that's how I wrote **VALIS.**

* * * * *

4-22-81

(We were discussing the failure of **Martian Time-Slip** to come out in hardcover)
GR: **VALIS** didn't come out in hardcover.
PKD: No, no hardcover publisher would buy **VALIS.** That's one thing that held it up before Bantam bought it, we tried for a couple of years to get a hardcover publisher. But that's more of the economics of the field at this point -- there's not much money.

Now (David) Hartwell of Simon and Schuster would not buy it. In fact he was here and he bought the sequel to **VALIS, The Divine Invasion.**
GR: You'd think they'd want both books.
PKD: (shrugs his shoulders)

(In September, talking about Hartwell's acceptance of **The Transmigration of Timothy Archer,** Phil told me that he'd refused to make changes in **VALIS** to please Hartwell or any other publisher. See Chapter 31.

(A manuscript exists of **VALIS System A,** the circa 1977 first version of the VALIS material, quite different I am told from the novel as finally published. Phil wrote it in a straight science fiction format. Hopefully it will some day be published).
GR: The movie, **VALIS,** within the book -- ?
PKD: Now, what film would you say that's based on?

(**VALIS,** the film-within-the-book, made in the book by a rock group).
GR: Well, it can't be **The Hindenburg!** (laughing. I think I was doing a pun on the rock group Led Zeppelin here.)
PKD: No, it's not **The Hindenburg.** I'm sure you know what film it's based on.
GR: The Man Who Fell to Earth (1977)?
PKD: Let's say I got the idea after seeing **The Man Who Fell to Earth.** I liked that a lot. And it gave me a chance to bring in the rock theme, because of (David) Bowie being in **Man Who Fell to Earth.**

* * * * *

(Phil told me a great deal about the vision of 1974 that provided the material for **VALIS.** This material forms a major portion of **Philip K. Dick: The Last Testament**).

CHAPTER 29
The Divine Invasion
"A Pleasure to Write"
A Sequel to VALIS
A Study of Judaism
Muzak and Linda Ronstadt

9-30-81

GR: Most recently published is **The Divine Invasion** (1981).
PKD: That was just plain pleasurable. I mean I had all the material in my mind. I'd done all that research on Judaism and I was just interested in the subject and the book was effortless to write. It was easily written, a pleasure to write

it was, and I just enjoyed every moment of it. It was a buoyant novel, it was full of life, and I was very, very happy at that point. I had felt **VALIS** was very successful -- we hadn't published it yet, but my agent told me he thought **VALIS** was a good book, well written, and I was just feeling real good. For the first time in my life I was able to live alone and enjoy it. It was written not out of desperation in isolation but in compatability with isolation. I was living alone but not suffering. I just wrote it and enjoyed it. I had a lot of fun writing it. No distractions 'cause I was living alone.

GR: I wanted to ask you about a point in it, the accident that the government "may have caused." It's left open.

PKD: Yes, there's no real evidence that it was done deliberately. In other words it may have been, but there's no evidence that it was. That is definately problematical. It's mere speculation that it was done by the government, and that was my intention. After all the government is not at issue. It may have been done by Belial working behind the scenes.

GR: The whole idea of the Catholic-Communist World Government is completely lost after they move over to the new world.

PKD: Well, those guys are no longer in power in the new world.

GR: They're appearing on TV talk-shows.

PKD: (laughs) The debased form of power is to be on TV talk-shows. This is based on my having watched (certain science-fiction writers) on TV talk-shows.

GR: Ever been on one?

PKD: No. And I ain't gonna be, either. They're gonna ask me how great a distance is a parsec, and I'm gonna say "What's a parsec?"

* * * * *

4-22-81

PKD: (The Divine Invasion) is the only sequel I've ever written to anything. I've never written a sequel before. It's a loose sequel. It doesn't follow immediately, it follows 200 years after **VALIS**. I figured if I had the Savior come back like in 1983 it would be pretty dumb. Have to scrap the book in a couple of years.

So I set it 200 years in the future. I don't even say, it's approximately 200 years in the future. It's obviously a whole new cast of characters, 'cause all the people in **VALIS** are **dead.**

There's this singer named Linda Fox (claps hands together). She's really great. And the whole novel is about this guy living on a dome on a colony planet, and all he does is listen to Linda Fox. God is a character in the book, and God arranges for him to meet Linda Fox. She's really great.

GR: There was a big gap between **Scanner** in 1977 and **VALIS** (published in February 1981) and now **The Divine Invasion.**

PKD: What happened was, it took Bantam forever to bring out **VALIS,** they held it a long time. Actually it took me a long time to write it and it took them a long time to publish it.

After I finished **VALIS** I started doing research into Judaism. **Valis Regained,** which was the title of the sequel - they changed it to **Divine Invasion** because they didn't want to get involved in Bantam's promotion of **VALIS.** Simon and Schuster wants to do their own promotions.

It's a hard cover book, $12.95, awful lot of money for a novel. Christ. I can't imagine paying $12.95 for a novel. Be that as it may --

I've switched from Christianity to Judaism. Christianity is renounced and denounced in the book. God is specifically Yahweh, as in the Old Testament. However - I soon wearied of the solemnity of Yahweh, and began to put in funny stuff. I could not control -- it's like **Galactic Pot Healer,** it got away from me. The guy's listening to Linda Fox tapes, God inserts scurrilous remarks in the tapes, changes the lyrics so they're real gross lyrics, and that's how God starts to communicate with him. I got into funny stuff on page 4. It's kind of a light-hearted view of Armageddon.

There are some very sad parts. The part where this little boy finds his dog has been run over on the road. The dog he so loved. Inasmuch as the little boy is God, he can talk to this dog, so he and the dog have this conversation, so the dog explains to him why he has been run over. It's got some good parts, some serious parts. By and large it's pretty light hearted. It's much lighter than all the ones (I've done lately).

It's already been reviewed. John Clute, who reviewed **VALIS** for the **Washington Post,** was able to get his hands - I don't know, he must have got a Xerox of the manuscript from the publishers - and read it and reviewed it. Now, and it won't be out till May or June. And he said it was a conventional novel. Which it is, very conventional.

But the study of Judaism that underlies it is very good. I didn't just rely on a cursory study of Judaism, I made a real study. To the point where I was thinking of converting to Judaism, I was so into it. I thought about nothing but Judaism for a couple of years. We're talking about several years here. **VALIS** was completed in '78, so I sent it off in '78. From then on I just worked on this thing, which is about Judaism. I studied the Torah. I don't read any Hebrew, but I had the Hebrew-English translation, with notes by the late chief rabbi of the British Empire, who was considered to be probably the most authoritative person in the English-speaking world on the Torah, and on Judaism. Joseph Campbell, for instance, considers him an authority.

I studied the Torah until I understood the underlying

themes of the Torah. I snuck in some Christianity. I finally got back to Christianity. It's inserted insidiously into the book. It's a Christian thing, which you would never identify as Christian. You would actually have to be something of a professional Christian, a scholar or something, to notice that Christianity has come in through the back door.

It's never identified as Christian either. It's the theme of exculpation from the punishment of the law, by surrogation. But so artfully concealed (in) claptrap, miserably inaccurate terms -- I go to some of the Greek words and retranslate them into English, so it comes out differently than to what we're accustomed to.

GR: I don't know what exculpation from the punishment, etc., is, really.
PKD: You haven't missed a thing. (laughs)

* * * * *

9-30-81

GR: What do you have against "Fiddler on the Roof?" (In **The Divine Invasion,** a character in suspended animation is made to listen to old Broadway show tunes for a near-eternity: a Muzak Purgatory).
PKD: I picked it arbitrarily. I love "Fiddler on the Roof." And "South Pacific.' I can't help it. I love both of them, and they came to mind.
GR: It's very funny.
PKD: "Fiddler" is ironic because of course that's about Jews and I'm very fond of it. It's very beautiful. I owned the album until I gave it to a girl who I knew was Jewish and we'd seen the picture together. So I really have nothing against it. Just awe because it's a Jewish thing and the book is about Judaism. But I did not mean to make it seem as if there was anything in "Fiddler" that was objectionable or jejune. I like it.

GR: Well, what you're objecting to is of course the soupy Muzak versions.
PKD: Yeah. I think now that I wish I had not used "Fiddler" because it is a more powerful --
GR: "South Pacific?"
PKD: The thing is those are about the only two that I'm really familiar with. I'm not familiar with the lesser (Broadway show scores).
GR: Have you heard from Linda Ronstadt?
PKD: No, but I'm sure I will tomorrow. (laughs) She just hasn't quite got around to reading my book yet.

* * * * *

I am waiting to hear from Linda Ronstadt, but there I am just teetering on the edge of psychosis. I don't think now that Linda's going to call me. But on the other hand I never did think that.
GR: You have a sort of claim on discovering her, I understand.
PKD: Well, that's a fantasy. I heard Linda Ronstadt sing years ago, when nobody had ever heard of Linda Ronstadt. And I thought she was the bee's knees. 'Cause I noticed that when she went to sing, she kicked off her shoes and looked straight down and didn't look at the audience. And I realized she was a very shy person, and I thought anybody that good who's that shy -- I just engrammed Linda Ronstadt.
GR: In **The Divine Invasion**, her song "You're No Good" is used as a negative.
PKD: I know, and I just hate that song. It's a bummer song. I don't think there should be a song where Linda repeats "You're no good, you're no good, you're no good." It's awful to be sitting in your living room making notes on your book, and hear somebody saying "you're no good" over and over again.

* * * * *

PART FOUR
The Last Year

CHAPTER 30
The Scott Meredith Agency / Discursive Writing / Russ Galen and Bishop Archer

10-12-81

PKD: I've had the same agent for 28 years, which is Scott Meredith. I've been represented at different times during that period by different sub-agents, that is people in his staff. The guy that represents me now is very, very good. He's one of the hottest agents in the world at this point. Russell Galen.

He was the one who showed me how to write **VALIS**. I would never have been able to write it without him. In correspondence with me he was able to tell me what were the strong points in my writing and what were the weak points. Also he expressed a great deal of confidence in my writing.

He saw as a strong point my discursive writing, the fact that I can cover a very large number of apparently unrelated things and draw them together into coherence. That I take off in all directions at once -- I can unify a tremendous diversity, and that gave me the idea for the structure of **VALIS,** which is tremendously discursive.

This is one of the great sins that you can commit these days in writing, is a very discursive book. Especially a subjective discursive book. You're supposed to stick to the plot, and you're supposed to write in the third person objective. And I wrote in the first person subjective, although I fudged that a little by writing about Horselover Fat. But I was tremendously subjective and tremendously discursive, and he gave me the courage to go and write a book like that.

He's been my agent for four or five years. He first showed up as my agent when **The Golden Man** collection came out (1980). He wrote me regarding the introduction to that, that it was the worst organized thing he'd ever read, and yet it was a work of genius. I thought an agent who is willing to tell you those two things in the same letter is not your standard agent. He is somebody else. He is quite different from the normal agent.

GR: You dedicated **VALIS** to him --

PKD: Oh, yes. Because he showed me how to do it.

I met him when he came out here. He's a real young guy. He looks just like I did when I was his age. He looks exactly like me. It's like looking at a photograph of me. It's incredible. The same forehead exactly as me. Everything.

Doesn't talk like me, though.

GR: In the **Golden Man** introduction you say you haven't met your agent in twenty-seven years. I presume you're talking about Scott Meredith.

PKD: Right. I'd never met anyone from the agency before, before Russ Galen came out here.

GR: How many other agents have you had, within the agency?

PKD: I don't know, because what they would do would be they'd all sign the name "Scott Meredith." It's only recently they started using their actual names. The previous one was very good, Jack Scocil was excellent. I'm not putting Scocil down, he did an awful lot for me, but Russ just really understands me. I can really depend on Russ to show me the direction I should go.

He is so gifted in understanding the strengths and weaknesses of a piece of writing. The man is so gifted -- the man is simply an analytical genius, his ability to take a work of writing, and show what is really good about it and what is really bad about it....

And he is very up front. He is tremendously honest, realistic and blunt. I called up one time, I had this plot idea for the Bishop Pike novel, and he said, "That's terrible.' And I was so excited I'd stayed up all night and called at 6 A.M. our time, 9 A.M. their time when he gets to work -- he wasn't even there yet. And I rattled off this plot idea, and he says it's awful. It's terrible! He didn't even hesitate. He didn't go through a polite number, working around to saying it's terrible. He just said forget it.

I said "Is it that bad?" and he said yes. And then he paused a moment and says, I gather you knew Bishop Pike. I said "Yes!" He says I gathered from your plot that you knew him on a personal basis. I said "Yes." He says, then don't write a plotted book about him. Write simply a book about him, and his life. Don't start out with this goddamn intricate plot thing you've developed. Write about your friend that's dead. Write all about him. Everything you remember.

And I did. And now Simon and Schuster has bought it and are bringing it out hard-cover. They were only going to bring it out paperback originally. All because of Russ!

GR: What was your original plot?

PKD: Oh, he's murdered by the government. 'Cause in my world the government is continually murdering everybody. Including my cats. And it's just dumb. It was this stupid thriller about this bishop who's in the civil rights stuff, and he gets offed by the government.

And Russ said, that's just stupid. First of all, nobody gives a shit about the '60s anymore and all that civil rights stuff and all that government intrigue, that's all a past number. Twenty million books like that have been written.

I says oh. 'Cause I don't read anything, except reference books. But then he showed me what to do, write about Bishop Pike as I knew him.

GR: I was going to ask about Bishop Pike, but I take it it's all in the book.

PKD: Well, the character is not Bishop Pike, the character is an original character, but it's based on Bishop Pike. Although I intended essentially to write about Bishop Pike I found that I was creating an original character when I wrote the book. And I did that in fact with the main character who's the protagonist, Angel Archer. She is totally fictitious.

* * * * *

CHAPTER 31
Writing Timothy Archer: The First Three Pages
A Woman as Protagonist
John Lennon's Death
Religious Mania
"My Poor Agent"
Harvey the Cat
Angel Archer
A Good Book

4-22-81

(Testing the machine to see if it was recording, I rewound and played a few words, and then ran it fast-forward to where our conversation had left off).
GR: Okay.
PKD: You cut me off in mid-sentence.
GR: No, I ran it forward.

PKD: Those were gems.

I had such a terrible time. I did this three pages on the new book (**The Transmigration of Timothy Archer,** which he was just beginning) -- it was just the rough draft, you know, and what I wanted to do was pass over from note taking to actual writing. (To) where I had actually shifted from the mode of note taking, which I had been doing forever and ever, into the mode of typing up a novel. It's very important to get down to where you write "Chapter One," you know, the first sentence.

And I worked myself into a complete cul-de-sac in three pages. And what was incredible was, that it took me twenty minutes to work myself into the cul-de-sac, and four hours to work myself out of it. Supposedly the best thing to do would be to just jettison the three pages, and do three other pages. But by that time I really liked those pages, and Paul (Williams said, which is more important, the whole novel or those three pages? And I says, well, at this point all I have are those three pages (laughing), you know the novel is theoretical but the pages are actual. I'm holding them in my hand.

He says, I like the first sentence. And I says, actually it does sort of go downhill after the first sentence.

I figured: Should I write this novel in a very experimental way? In a really outrageous way. And I thought, it'll be pretentious. Here I am writing a literary novel, and I have this big thought balloon over my head the whole time, "I am writing a **literary** novel," the word "literary" is all lit up in huge letters.

So I go, I will write like Raymond Chandler, or somebody like that. I'll write a spare, economical prose, you know, very sparse.

So the first page tells you where you are, when you are, and who the protagonist is. A "where when what" scene, what she's doing. (The protagonist) is a woman.

I did this because Ursula LeGuin said, in public, down in Atlanta, Georgia, that she couldn't abide **VALIS** -- she couldn't abide any of my recent writing -- because all the women are hateful. Well, that means she didn't read the **Playboy** story ("Frozen Journey," 1980), because the woman in there is very, very loving, and very, very tender and giving. And I wrote her a slip and told her that, and she, she --

But I felt, that presents a challenge to me now. Suppose I write from the viewpoint of a woman, just to prove that I'm not a misogynist. I'll write it from the standpoint of a woman.

So then I have this difficult literary task on my hands, I might as well compound the problem by writing from the standpoint of a woman. I write it from the standpoint of a young woman, 'cause I'll even have an age difference, like I'm 52 and she'll be 21.

But then I forgot that she couldn't be married when "Rubber Soul" came out (laughs), that was 1966 and the novel is set the day John Lennon is shot. That's when it starts out.

GR: Is the whole novel set in that one day?

PKD: Jeez, I hope not! (laughs) I think I'm going to have to do flashbacks, because --

Well of course I have to do flashbacks, Lennon's only been dead for a couple of months, everything would have to happen --

GR: You could write it into the future.

PKD: Then it would become science fiction!

You know, I was saying to Paul, you know Paul, it's amazing, in a mnemonic novel - that's present-day setting - you can't just move around in time and space like you can in a science fiction novel. And he says, (emphasizing each word) Yes, Phil, That's Correct. If you say she was married in 1966, you don't then get to say she was in high school in

1966. You have to make choices in realistic novels you don't make in science fiction. (In) science fiction you can do all this self-contradictory stuff.

So it's going to have to be handled with flashbacks. Either that or I'm going to have to jettison the opening, where she's walking up the gangplank of a houseboat in Sausalito to sit in on a seminar on Sufi mysticism. And she's wondering what the fuck she's doing that for, the day John Lennon was shot. And I just love that opening. (He kept it).

So he said, Paul said (laughing) why don't you have it the day Otis Redding died, set it back in I don't know, 1978. Or Jim Morrison. Croce. Joplin! I could set it back -- Jimi Hendrix.

She could be thinking, Jimi Hendrix is dead, and here I am walking onto a houseboat in Sausalito, to listen to a lecture on Sufis. What am I doing this for? I wish I'd thought of that at 11:30 last night. I was sitting there till 4 a.m. scratching out words. I had to jettison a whole character, the guy she was married to. I had to edit him out. He no longer exists. That cuts me down from 15 to 14 characters. But with that many characters, who's going to know the difference?

GR: Is it going to be another multi-viewpoint novel, like **Crap Artist?**

PKD: No, it's all going to be from her viewpoint. I'm just abandoning everything I've ever done. It's first person interior. Well, I'm not abandoning everything I've ever done, because that's how **Crap Artist** and **VALIS** start out.

A young woman, walks into a record store in Berkeley, has been married -- I says to Paul, all the characters in the book are 115 years old, according to my chronology. (laughs) I'm stuck with my own premise. My irreversible premise.

It's about a bishop who becomes intoxicated with the fervor of religious zeal. And it leads him to madness and death. In other words, he's taken over by Dionysus.

I read an article a number of years ago called "Dionysus in America," by a very fine English critic, and his analysis of the '60s was that Dionysus had epiphanized in the United States, (that) somewhere between Woodstock and Altamont, Dionysus took over the counter-culture. And the article is very convincing.

This book will be an analysis of religious mania. In a way it's a reaction to **VALIS.** It's another viewpoint on the religious mania in **VALIS.** But it's a much more negative viewpoint, much much more hostile than the viewpoint that I as a character had in **VALIS** toward Horselover Fat. This is completely negative. It leads to madness and death, and it leads to madness and death in person after person after person.

The bishop, his son, and his mistress all die. First the son, by suicide, then the mistress, by suicide, then the bishop dies in Israel, looking for the place where the Zadokite Scroll was found. He thinks the Zadokite Scrolls give the true origin of Christianity. -- I made this up, there is no Zadokite sect, but there was a priest named Zadok, and there were Zadokite scrolls found, you know, the Dead Sea scrolls. These scrolls in my novel date from 200 B.C., and they prefigure the Christian sacraments, and they prefigure a lot of what Jesus said. So he immediately leaps to the conclusion that he's found the true origins of Christianity, and at that point jettisons his whole career as a bishop, and his whole belief in Christ. His whole conviction that the Zadokites were the true religion just destroys himself and everyone around him...It costs him his life, finally.

And the girl is the wife of the bishop's son. She was his girlfriend, and not his wife, until last night, but now she's his wife because I screwed up on those first three pages. God, you'd think I'd chisel them in granite or something.

(Through the spring and into the early summer of 1981, Phil Dick continued writing **The Transmigration of Timothy Archer.** Its later history was related to me by mail. In a letter dated June 26, 1981, he wrote that he had just finished the novel, writing the final 90 pages in two days, and then sent it off to dead silence from the office of his publisher, David Hartwell, in New York. Yet he was very proud of it, and how he'd carried off the character of Angel Archer.

(Three days later, on June 29, he wrote me again to say that Hartwell had accepted the book, much to his joy. -- The texts of both of these letters, slightly amended, comprises Appendix C of this book.

(By late September, when we met again, production on publication of the novel was well advanced).

9-30-81

(As the recorder was turned on):
PKD: Now as to my sins.
...My poor agent, he worked one week copyreading the manuscript of the Bishop Timothy Archer novel. On his own time, at home, every night. And he's very thorough. Much more thorough than I would have been. What I do is just go through it like you go through the phone book, you know, just thumb through it real fast. I'm bad at that. And I'm so tired now that if I had tried to do it - had I been able to do it - I would have done a poor job. I literally could not have done a good job.

I had told him, I said, there's no use in sending me a manuscript. They put it right into production! It seems like I just finished it last week. It seems like I just sent it off. I just sent it off, and it's already in production. And the reason is, they want to bring it out next May, so it had to go into production right away. And curiously enough next May is when the "Road Runner" film comes out....

* * * * *

I haven't heard a great deal from Simon and Schuster. They don't talk a lot. They don't call you up and babble at you. Even their acknowledgement that the manuscript was satisfactory came by mail, they didn't phone me up and tell me. Something that important -- if it were me I would have phoned the author to tell him that. But then authors are always making this complaint. They want good news quick and bad news slow. And editors just tend to write letters.

And it was just one sentence. "We found the novel excellent and it was quite satisfactory," you know. And I just deduced that that meant we had a binding agreement, that the novel satisfied the contract. And that is correct, it did. Because Hartwell had said originally that he would probably ask for revisions. He made it clear that he would expect me to at least seriously consider revising it were he to suggest it.

Because he had seen **VALIS,** and he had been told correctly by my agent that I would **not** change **VALIS.** I told my agent, I will not change **VALIS.** And my agent had reported that.

(To his cat, who is sticking his head inside my carry-bag for the tape recorder): Put it in his bag, and then we'll seal the bag up and then throw it down the trash. (To me) One intrviewer was here with a satchel, and (the cat) stuck his head in the satchel, and I thought any animal who sticks his head in a satchel--! Darwin would have something to say about that. (laughter) You're not going to survive in the wild! What are you going to do without me, Harvey, when I'm gone? You won't be able to forage. (Phil's fat and lazy cats are being taken care of by his last wife, Tessa).

(Phil went on to tell how his agent had answered some 98% of the 1,400 questions Simon and Schuster had about his manuscript, and how he had fielded the rest).

PKD: So I rewarded my agent by sending him airfare. He wants to come out for the gala premiere of **Blade Runner**. I figured that's the least I can do.

* * * * *

10-12-81

(Phil had been speaking of the pain he felt in separation from his children)

PKD: On the other hand, though, when I finished the Bishop Timothy Archer novel, the new one, when I created the character of Angel Archer as my protagonist, when I got finished writing that book and had to stop writing from her viewpoint - and it's all interior first person, relentlessly so, so that there's no other viewpoint but her interior viewpoint, her thoughts, her mind - I felt a loss as real as I have ever felt. In fact I went into a spiral-down, psychologically, when that moment came, when I began to realize that I would never ever be in the mind of Angel Archer, or put another way, Angel Archer's mind would never be in mine. Our minds would never be one mind again.

And even reading the book would not bring that back, when her mind and my mind were one mind. I was in syzergy with this woman. This incredibly funny, brilliant, sane, warm, wise, rational person, with all her little hangups and all her little mischievous tricks - like when she's visiting her friend in the hospital she says, I always made sure I brought her something she couldn't eat or something she couldn't wear - you get this sense of the spirit, this incredible spirit of Angel Archer.

I just suffered. I suffered as much when I finished that book as I have from having relationships break up. I lost a human friend when I finished that book. It was **awful**. And one time I was driving my car, and I said, I'm going to pretend I'm Angel Archer, 'cause she used to drive her car differently from me. She'd go tearing around in this little Honda Civic, just real great, and just go through yellow lights. People would say, goddamn it Angel, you're going to roll that tin can one of these days. And I says, I'm going to pretend I'm Angel Archer and I drove for awhile as Angel Archer. That's kind of fun.

She has this deadpan humor. People tell her things that are absurd, that they believe in very firmly. And instead of saying to them you're full of shit or something like that, she says something which is absolutely sarcastic but in no way does it sound sarcastic. It's just an incredible way of responding which I can't do. I have no capacity to do that. She does things that I can't do. She's so smart. So wise.

And then she just fucks up terribly in the book. She makes a ghastly mistake, just an incredible mistake, that costs the Bishop his life. He comes to her before he goes to Israel and says, Angel, you know I'm a lousy driver, right? And she says, yeah, right. He says, you're a real good driver, right? He says, I want you to go to Israel with me to drive the car there, when I rent a car. Because if you don't I'll die there.

And she says, Tim, you're being neurotic. She says I have my own life here, I'm running a record store, you know, I can't take off here from my life in Berkeley. And then he says to her, you're a professional student. You can't break away from life in Berkeley. You've got to do it, it's for your sake too. You and I have both got to go to Israel, for your sake and for my sake. And she says you're wrong in both cases. You'll be okay and I'll be okay.

He goes to Israel, he backs over a rock, gets the rear end hung up and dies in Israel, and then she realizes that the other part is true too -- that she is welded fast to Berkeley forever, for life. She will never now leave Berkeley. She will be a professional student all of her life. So she has killed her friend and she has killed herself. And the moment she realizes this she dies spiritually. It's simply the death of her soul at that moment. That's one of the great passages in literature, is her realization of what his death means for her.

It isn't that she goes on a guilt trip. It isn't that she spends the rest of her life saying, oh, if only I'd gone to Israel. She does say that from time to time, but she's too sane to be caught up in a neurotic spiral like that. But what is not neurotic is her realization that she's ossified. And that Bishop Archer was right, when he told her she was ossified. Because as much as she loves the bishop, she is a little patronizing to him, because he is a fuck-up...In this case, the bishop was right and she was wrong. She's right 99% of the time but she's wrong once, and as a result two people die. He dies physically and she dies spiritually. A great, great character and a great, great human being.

(The scenes with Bishop Archer trying to talk Angel into going to Israel with him, and his and her consequent deaths all take place in chapter 13 of the completed novel. They are every bit as good as Phil claimed they were. For a discussion of the wonderful scenes of Angel's rebirth which conclude the novel see his letter to me of June 26, 1981, in Appendix C).

(At this point we returned to the topic of the novel being like a child of his).

PKD: Then why am I living alone in this apartment with two mangy cats?....What are my rewards for it? You get to read the book, what do I get? I get about a hundred dollars for doing the book, they pay me such a little amount for it.

They said, look, we'll be honest with you. This is all up-front. Simon and Schuster said, look. If you write a literary novel we'll pay you one third of what we'll pay you for a science fiction novel. You've lost two-thirds of your income right there. Do you want to take it?

I said, yes I do. I want to do it. And I did it. And it was a good book.

(Simon and Schuster paid Philip K. Dick $7,500 for his novel, **The Transmigration of Timothy Archer.** They apparently contracted, however, at the same time to pay him three times as much for a science fiction novel, **The Owl in Daylight,** which he did not live to complete.

(**The Transmigration of Timothy Archer** was published after Philip K. Dick's death, and received good to very good reviews.)

* * * * *

CHAPTER 32

The Making of Blade Runner / Ridley Scott / "I Won't Do The God-Damned Novelization" / Rewriting a "Joke Screenplay" / "They Did Sight Stimulation on My Brain" / Good Grass / Science Fiction as Futurism / "I Was Ecstatic" / My Little Boy A Near-Great Film

(Over the last year of his life, Phil Dick followed - first with mistrust, and then with a growing if hard-earned admiration - the making of the Warner Brothers-Ladd Company-Ridley Scott film **Blade Runner,** loosely adapted from his 1968 novel **Do Androids Dream of Electric Sheep?** The saga of Phil's conflicting emotions over the project can be followed in his comments over a period of months, to me and to others who interviewed him.

(When I first talked to Phil in April 1981 I had just heard about the film, then being photographed, and was quite excited. It was up to Phil to disillusion me):

4-22-81

GR: What do you think of Ridley Scott? Did you like **Alien?**
PKD: No, I didn't like **Alien,** and I said so and he knows it. I said a spaceship is a spaceship and a monster is a monster. All it was was special effects, the best monster anybody ever -- (H.R.) Giger I think did the monster.
GR: A beautiful monster.
PKD: Oh yeah, if you like monsters, but conceptually the idea --
GR: The idea is horrible.
PKD: There's no ideation in the film. And I said that in the article I wrote for SelecTV. (A short non-fiction piece called "Universe Makers...and Breakers" Phil wrote for the cable system's **SelecTV Guide**, Feb. 15, 1981). And they (the film company) called me up, and started yelling at me on the phone.
GR: Who called you up?
PKD: The **Blade Runner** people. I was saying dangerous things. But they have turned my book into a simple action story, androids killing humans and humans killing androids.
GR: Is it really? That's the main thing I wanted to know, if it was a serious adaptation.
PKD: Not it's not. It's called "loosely adapted." And it will be very spectacular because they have Douglas Trumbull doing the special effects. So I'm sure the total impact graphically and visually will be dynamite.

But. (long pause) There's a long story that goes with this, but I can reduce it to a few words. They want to do a novelization based on the screenplay, which is quite often the case. They were going to have somebody do it, and they had to get my permission. And my agent and I refused to allow them to do it. We said we were going to reissue the original novel.

So they came back with an offer to have me do the novelization. They would take me up to Hollywood, and I would sit in on the filming, and I'd be impressed, you know, God!, my eyes would be like saucers. I'd look like Mr. Toad when he saw the first motorcar. And I'd meet Ridley Scott, and then do the novelization. They'd make a deal and cut us in on the merchandise, and they'd do this and this.

And my agent was figuring on how much this'd get me. He figured out that I'd make about $400,000. I says, I don't want to do this. I want to write this novel about Bishop Timothy Archer, the one I'm working on.

So David Hartwell from Simon and Schuster flew out to talk to me about that. And he read the outline (of **Timothy Archer**), and he said "I'll buy it. But I can't give you very much." So he goes back to New York, and my agent calls me yesterday and he says, they'll give you $7,500 for the Timothy Archer literary novel. Or you can make $400,000 doing this novelization based on the screenplay.

I says, I won't do the goddamned novelization. I don't want the $400,000. I do want to do this novel about Timothy Archer. My agent says, "Fine. I'm going to the Nebula Awards at the end of the week. I'm going to take Judy Lynn Del Rey and I'm going to tell every writer that I see that you turned down $400,000 to write a $7,500 literary novel. Because I want every writer at that convention to know that, that you turned down $400,000."

I says, well, I don't have any use for the $400,000 anyway. He says "I'm not going to tell them that. I'm just going to say most writers are whores, and you're not a whore." It's as simple as that. And he quoted that thing by George Bernard Shaw, that famous thing Shaw says, where he said to this woman, Would you sleep with this particular guy for five million pounds? And she says of course. And he says, Would you sleep with him for five pounds? She says of course not, I'm not a whore. He says, Madame, I've already established you're a whore. It's just a question of figuring out what your price is.

So anyway, the **Blade Runner** people are now really angry at me...

(They're making it up in Hollywood, on sound stages). They've built a hovercraft, they built one that flies. It actually takes off. They've got a designer from Detroit. Damnedest thing. Haven't seen it, but I've heard it's real good.

It cost six million dollars to do all this. Pre-production art. But a joke screenplay.

GR: I take it you didn't have anything to do with the screenplay.

PKD: They never said a word to me and they never told me. I had an awful time getting ahold of the screenplay. They only gave it to me after everything was set up. I didn't even know they were making the film until somebody told me about it, congratulated me. He'd read it in the trades.

GR: I take it you're not getting much for the rights.

PKD: I wish I had a percentage of the gross, but I don't. I got paid a cash sum that was pretty good, but I don't have any points. It was brokered, see, it was bought by some very small operators and they went out and brokered it up to Michael Deely. Deely was able to bring everybody (else) in. So then it escalated.

GR: Did you see **The Duellists** (1978)? -- It was Ridley Scott's first film.

PKD: No.

GR: It had a very good, very intelligent, very literate script.

PKD: That's right, you're into films.

GR: I am.

PKD: Did you see (Robert) Altman's **3 Women** (1977)?...I liked that a lot. Unbelievable.

* * * * *

9-30-81

(We were talking about **Timothy Archer** and its publication date)

PKD: They want to bring it out next May. And curiously enough next May is when the "Road Runner" film comes out, or whatever it's called. Is that what it's called?

GR: Blade Runner.

PKD: Blade Runner! Yes, of course. Why did I say "Road Runner?" This is why I'll be no good in going over names (in copyreading **Timothy Archer**).

No, I've been calling it "Road Runner." It's like what Frank Herbert once said, the sequel to **Dune** is **Dune Buggy.**

But it all got to be too much for me. It's like Carrie Snodgress's movie, when she's playing **Diary of a Mad Housewife,** and all of a sudden the ironing board and the shopping in the supermarket got to be too much for her.

In dealing with Hollywood I was dealing with power brokers for the first time in my life. It took me a long time to come up with that term, because that's what it is. It isn't rich people, it's powerful people. I mean, I've known wealthy people before. Wealth confers power automatically.

But these people are real **power** brokers. They buy and sell human beings. It's like it says in the Bible about Babylon, they sell pearl, ivory, and the souls of men. And this is exactly what is going on in Hollywood, they deal with the souls of human beings.

The **Blade Runner** people finally found a real nice guy to handle me, because it was evident that I was really intractable. I mean I could not be dealt with by the normal methods. What I woud do would be to simply withdraw, and then write a scathing article or letter, and fire it off, and **hide** when the thing came out.

So they sent down a real nice guy. He came down, he was wearing jeans and stuff like that. He was very informal. He had read the book, he had read my novel. Which really made a difference, because the whole thing with Ridley Scott, he's alleged to have said "I could not read the novel" - once I heard **that,** I was programmed for a head-on collision with Hollywood after that. That probably is the worst thing I could have heard. If anything is guaranteed to create a schism between me and Hollywood it would be that the director of the film had not and would not and could not read the novel.

Once that started it was in for a penny, in for a pound. I was angry, and I was frightened by what I was going to see come out of that. Since he would be filming a film based on a book he had not read -- that's pretty scary. That's pretty scary to the author. It may not be scary to him, but it's scary to me. Because I don't see how it could possibly resemble my book under those circumstances. He in essence would have repudiated my book from the beginning.

Now, the guy they brought in (as screenwriter for a rewrite of the film), David W. Peoples, he went back to the book, and he studied the book, and he transfered the essential thematic material of the book, he didn't transfer all of the elements, because that's not practical. That's not how it's done. You know that, don't you? It's not done item by item, like that play of **Nicholas Nickleby** in New York that runs something like eight hours, that's every word in every scene.

Peoples is also an excellent writer as well as a serious writer and a reputable writer. He just did a great job on the screenplay.

And yet they didn't show me the screenplay that he did. They showed me the earlier one, before he was brought in. And all the negotiations to have me do a novelization were based on me having seen a screenplay that would not be used, rather than the much better screenplay that was used.

Now - I asked myself, was this just carelessness on their part? There's three possibilities - just carelessness on their part; or a fear of industrial piracy on their part, which is very possible, that they did not want their actual shooting script to get out, and they wanted it noised about that they had a poor screenplay, because everyone would be convinced that it would not be worth stealing -- there's always that fear that a quickie TV movie would be made real fast. Or -- it's possible that they did not know how much better the final screenplay was. There's always that possibility. They literally did not know, A, how bad the original screenplay was, and B, how good the Peoples version was.

In any case, when I read his version I just flipped out it was so good, and I called them up and just raved, and then they sent the guy down here, Jeff Walker. And he was so nice. He brought me photos...

(At this point Phil showed me photos of the **Blade Runner** production, providing a running commentary. Among other things I learned that someone had told Dick that he'd invented the word "hovercraft" in his original **Androids** novel -- "I don't know if I've patented it or not, maybe I have a copyright on that word. Someday I'll look into that if I ever need any money. Wouldn't it be great to get royalties? Everytime they built a hovercraft they had to pay you."

("I didn't go up for the filming," he told me. "I still feared for my soul." He said that the film's coinage of "replicants" as opposed to "androids" was a "good word." And Sean Young as Rachel -- "It's like they took my brain out and did sight stimulation on my brain, so it projected an image on the screen. That's exactly how I pictured her. If you'd laid out a hundred photographs of a hundred women I could have unerringly picked that one out, because that's Rachel. She's perfect.")

(Phil also added a few more details to his renunciations of a fortune in not writing a novelization of the **Blade Runner** screenplay. -- Unfortunately I didn't think to ask if he'd have been more tempted to do one for the Peoples screenplay instead of "Eat lead, robot!" version - as he once referred to it - he refused. Pointing to a photo of Harrison Ford as Rick Deckard, he noted the "Phillip Marlowe look" and said --)

PKD: Raiders of the Lost Ark, the book (novelized screenplay), was Number 8 on the best seller list. That's where I could have made a million dollars if I'd done the novelization. That's another reason it would have been terrifying if my literary novel had not been publishable, because I would have been rich on the novelization of the screenplay. I literally would never have to work for the rest of my life.

But on the other hand that doesn't appeal to me particularly. I work for pleasure and not for profit anyway. God knows it has had to have been that way!

* * * * *

10-12-81

(After the angry speech recorded in Chapter 31 about how little he was paid for writing **Timothy Archer**, we took a break. When the recorder was flipped on again, Phil was in a completely different mood -- though not for the reason he indicates!)

PKD: You want to save the roaches, or shall we just swallow them?

(adopting a stoned voice) Oh, boy, that was good grass. Ah, Gregg, listen, you've got to cut down, man. That period there where you were trying to put the phonograph record on the cat's post -- you're really fucked up, man. The phonograph is over that way. No, no, stop looking at the ceiling. It's not on the ceiling.

Do you have anything to say in your defense?
GR: I'll be doing the writing, so I can put in anything I want.
PKD: Power of the press, huh?

Last night I got a phone call from a friend, up in the Bay Area. And he says, Hey! Your movie's on ABC-TV, a program called "Hooray for Hollywood." So I ring off real fast, and I check it and it's on an hour later down here than it is in the Bay Area.

So I say, hot dog. I've seen about two seconds of **Blade Runner,** that's all I've seen. Literally. Plus some stills.

So I sit there in front of the set. They do a couple of other films. They're talking about the economics of making a picture. They go into **The Stunt Man,** which was critically acclaimed but a box office failure, and then "Doorway to Heaven" -- is that the name of it?...**Heaven's Gate.** "Doorway to Summer," **Heaven Can Wait** -- it's got "Heaven" in it somewhere. (Phil makes a reference here to Robert Heinlein's **The Door Into Summer**).

All of a sudden on the screen appears not footage of **Blade Runner,** but footage of them filming **Blade Runner,** which is what I was supposed to go up and see, see, but I didn't do because I was working on that damn literary novel.

And they had numerous freaks walking around in Mohawk haircuts. And these were not actors, these were actual punk rock people that they had cattle-called in. They were real! And the air was all mucked up with mist and haze and smoke and grit and dirt, and all these garish neon signs. And the scene was real short. Harrison Ford is jumping down from someplace onto the sidewalk. But there are so many of these weirded-out people, that it takes a long time for him to find an empty spot amongst this milling throng to hop down.

That's all it consists of. And they yell "cut," and he kind of threads his way amongst the people. And I'm looking at this, and then they interview him. They interviewed him right there at the set as he came off, and they ask him, how do you feel about making another space fantasy? And he says, this is not a space fantasy. Do you know what this is? This is futurism. This is the way it **is** going to be. Those other films (**Star Wars**), that's not how it's going to be.

I suddenly realized he was right. It isn't even science fiction. Because science fiction does not really try to predict the future. That is a fact. It's not debatable. That is not the role of science fiction, to predict the future. Science fiction books and stories are not judged on whether they come true or not. Because if that were the case there'd be one science fiction book. The right one.

And I thought, by God, these guys have figured out what life is going to be like forty years from now. My God! I'm completely convinced. This is a new art form. It's like time travel. It's like everything that you hate about urban life now, escalated to the level of Dante's **Inferno**. It was just awful. He couldn't even find room to hop down on the sidewalk. You can't even run in the future, there's so many people milling around, doing nothing.

And there's millions of signs, information everywhere, do this, buy that. Half of it's in Chinese, or some strange alphabet. It was so real, that I had the feeling that they had created a new art form. Literally created a new art form. And I was like, ecstatic. I wrote a letter to the production company, and I drove up at two o'clock in the morning and delivered it to the main post office, so they'd get it tomorrow.

It was so invigorating. In reading over my novel, they

must have grasped that underneath the adventure - the cops, the robbers, the chase and so on - that there was a certain element of realism in that book and they drew on that, as well as the adventure. This is not just a cop killing a bunch of replicants. This is not like anything we have ever seen, and this is **not** aimed at 12-year-olds.

It wasn't written for 12 year olds. It isn't like anything that has ever been done. These people set out literally to figure out what L.A. would be like forty years from now. They could be wrong -- for instance the Third World War could break out, in which case there wouldn't be any L.A. at all. But it's like that thing that Heinlein says, "If this goes on..." If the trends that we have now -- this is a projection, like computer projection. It is going to be exactly like that. It's like everything we have now only worse. That detective could hardly walk across the street...

I can't claim all that (much) credit. I will claim some credit for it. I'd be an idiot to take no credit! So I will take some credit. How much is justifiably mine I don't know. I don't know how much David W. Peoples went to my book for, when he came in. And I don't know how much Syd Mead, when he did the pre-production art, went to my book for. Or Douglas Trumbull, when he did the special effects. I don't know. All I know is that Ridley Scott said he couldn't read the book, that doesn't prove the others didn't.

(The evidence is inconclusive. According to the definitive "making of the film" articles in **Cinefantastique,** July-August 1982, and **Cinefex** 9, July 1982, Mead, Trumbull, and the many other artisans involved in creating the look of the film drew principally from designs and ideas sketched by Scott himself, a commercial artist before he became a film maker. On the other hand, Scott may have been influenced more than he knew by the Dick material as filtered through the various screenplays...The essence of Phil Dick is hard to dilute and easy to be intoxicated by).

How do I know if Harrison Ford's read that book? It's not something I can say that I know Harrison Ford read that book, and knows what kind of person I've projected Rick Deckard to be -- but I had the sense that he had read the book. He just seemed to be Rick Deckard.

...Harrison Ford **is** Rick Deckard. You would almost accuse me of having written the character based on Harrison Ford, that it worked that way. It's a good movie and it's going to be a big hit. It's going to make a mint. They're going to be rich.

GR: How many points do you have in the film?

PKD: I've got none. Zero points, that's exactly what I've got in the film. And every time they sell one of them action figures, you know, that's money out of my pocket as I could have gotten 10%. (If he had written the novelization, he might have been brought into the merchandising promotions, which as it was failed to develop in any significant way -- the film did not make back its enormous, upwards of $22 million cost, in its initial release).

My little boy will be coming home with a pile of that stuff. In fact, I showed him the article in the new **Rolling Stone** (a brief promo for the film)...I says, Hey, Christopher! Look at this! See, that's Harrison Ford, look! 'Cause he has the Han Solo action toy. And he's always playing with the "Maltese Flacon" or whatever that goddamn thing is called -- what it's called?

GR: "The Millenium Falcon."

PKD: Ah, yeah -- And I said, Hey, look Christopher, see Daddy's name there and see Harrison Ford.

"Uh huh," he says. (indicating complete lack of interest. Phil laughs) We'll go to see it next year, and halfway through he'll say, "Can we leave now?" I know how kids feel. I know you won't believe this but I was once a kid.

* * * * *

(Although we talked on the phone after this, we never

conversed on tape on **Blade Runner** again. Two later interviews, by Paul Sammon in **Cinefantastique,** and John Boonstra in **Twilight Zone,** June 1982, supply more detail on Phil's later reactions to the project.

(In December of 1981 Phil was shown twenty minutes of rough-cut footage by Ridley Scott himself, and was quite impressed. I recall Phil telling me on the phone that "I said my piece and Ridley Scott said his piece and that was that." Sammon provides more details of the two men's "cordial" talk. A photo I've seen of their meeting - Phil had it pinned on his wall, together with some other **Blade Runner** stills, when I last saw him in February - shows Phil full of bravado, head cocked to one side and smiling, while Scott looks rather nonplussed.

(Phil died without ever seeing any more of the film. Although he assured me that his name would be featured in the credits, that it was in his contract to be so, it is in fact not, although a dedication to him can be seen if you wait through all of the final credits.

(The film, I think, is a near-masterpiece, Scott's dizzyingly dense texture providing a superb background for a strong story of yearning masochistic romance, all fairly well permeated with a Phil Dick sensibility. This though many of the story's more original touches - the built-in obsolescence of the androids, or "replicants," which gives their quest to live such poignance, being most important here - were apparently contributed by David Peoples. Dick thought vey highly of People's rewrite of the showdown, in which Roy Baty, the dying replicant, lets his foe Rick Deckard live. This, he told Sammon, was "wonderful" and "moving."

(Interestingly, two of the problems with **Blade Runner** as it now stands were pinpointed by Phil in his pre-release interviews. He told me that Scott had shot three endings to the film, joking that at the Hollywood preview of the film he planned to go to in the spring, the audience would be handed cards and get to vote on the ending they preferred. He also told Sammon that one of the main problems with the original, pre-Peoples screenplay was the "cliche-ridden Chandleresque" voice-over narration provided Deckard.

(The film as shot and previewed contained no voice-overs and ended with Rachel's fate left unresolved, an elevator door closing on her face. --An improvement, Phil considered, over the original script's device of having Rachel kill herself for Deckard's own good. There is some controversy over exactly who is responsible -- Andrew Sarris' **Village Voice** review of the film, July 5, 1982, alludes to rumors of Ridley Scott's being fired at one point -- but apparently, in a panic move, a last-minute narration was added to "explain" the film to puzzled viewers, and an idiotic happy ending cobbled on. This ending consists of outtakes of Stanley Kubrick's **The Shining** (1980), helicopter shots of mountain scenery, into which shots of a grinning Rick & Rachel have been cut in, his narration explaining that, oh yeah, the replicant's planned obsolescence had been skipped when they built her. Judging from interviews, Scott apprently did shoot this new footage, and as far as I'm concerned the dopey narration - "What's happening to me?" - and the silly ending still sort of work, so powerful is so much of the rest of the film. The narration makes me feel so sorry for Deckard, this down at the heels "blade runner" from this run-down future, that if he and his mechanical bride want to hie off to the Overlook Hotel for their honeymoon, it's okay by me.

(The important thing, in the long run, is that Phil saw enough of the movie to know that it was, after all, nearly enough of a great film that its flaws don't really matter. When all is said and done, giving all the credit they deserve to Scott and Peoples and (co-scenarist) Hampton Fancher, and Trumbull and Mead and the technical crew, what millions of people responded to when they saw **Blade**

Runner was to a large degree a reflection of the spirit of Philip K. Dick).

* * * * *

CHAPTER 33
The Owl in Daylight

(Phil's letter to me of June 29, 1981 - published in Appendix C - refers at some length to his "novel-in-progress," **The Owl in Daylight,** which as a science fiction novel his publisher, David Hartwell, was paying him three times as much as he did for his straight, literary novel, **The Transmigration of Timothy Archer.** What he wrote in that letter and what he told me here is to my knowledge all that he said about the book, parts of which at least I hope exist written down somewhere. --Paul Williams, executor of the Dick estate, tells me he hasn't found a page.

(Unfortunately Phil, with this last, unwritten, novel seemed to be following in the writing habits that had served him well so long, which was to work everything out in his head before much got committed to paper. And as he told me in succeeding months he never could sit down at the typewriter and put down what was in his head. He was tired, he was ill, the shadow of death drew closer, and his energies burned away in his last visions and enthusiasms: the suffering Tagore, the returning Maitreya.

(I am putting what Phil had to say, with such power and eloquence, about his final religious and philosophical epiphanies in the next book of this series, **Philip K. Dick: The Last Testament.** But here is where I am placing what Phil had to say about his last book, the one he never wrote):

9-30-81

GR: You have something in mind for your next novel?
PKD: It's all worked out. I was starting on it. I had gotten down to the minor characters. The next thing to do was to sit down at the typewriter -- and I just fell flat on my face. I could not lift my hands. I could not go from the notes to the typewriter. I had everything. The plot, the theme, the characters -- **everything!** And I just crapped out.
GR: When do you think you'll get back to it?
PKD: I told my agent it could be a week, a month, or it could be forever. I may never write another book again, seriously. That might be it.

What I did was I sat down, and tried to think of the most ambitious science fiction novel I could write. Because I had written a literary novel, and I didn't want to go back to writing formula science fiction, or genre science fiction, whatever you want to call it. And then having done so -- like, you know the thing, can God create a ditch so wide He can't jump over it, well, can I create a challenge of theme and plot so great that when I went to write it, I couldn't write it -- Yes. The answer's yes. I was definitely able to envision a novel of such complexity and depth and importance that when I went to write it I couldn't even type "page one" on the page.

I was talking to a friend the other night about it, and he said, look what you're proposing to do. The character is based on Beethoven, and the plot is based on Goethe's **Faust.** Beethoven and Goethe's **Faust**, can't understand why you can't write it! He said, I accuse you of being your own character. In the book the character has reached the end of the Third Period - which is what Beethoven did and died - and he wants to go into a Fourth Period - and to do that, he's got to surmount the first three periods.

So I had to figure out what Beethoven's Fourth Period would have consisted of. And that broke me. That broke me to try to think of it. I studied the first three periods, and tried to project a fourth period, and in projecting it, I broke the projector, which is my own brain. I was able to conceive of it, but then I just passed out.

GR: Didn't you tell me that what Beethoven's next period would have been comes out in one movement of one of his last quartets?

PKD: Yes, I was thinking of the 13th Quartet...but I don't see that as telling me anything. I project something different.

I had the chance of writing a conventional (s.f.) novel and actually writing it, or conceiving of an incredibly important masterpiece, and not being able to write it at all, and I chose the latter. It's like a Greek myth. (laughter)

GR: If your mind can conceive of it, and you have all the plot worked out - that's the hard part, isn't it? - the

transcription should be relatively easy.
PKD: Well, I thought so. That was my impression. (chuckling) But when the moment came to go to the typewriter, I suddenly realized I had nothing left. I was out of orgone.
GR: All I can say is, you have to write it. This is your Fifth Period. I'm going to be in print, committed to predicting a great new period of writing for you, and you can't let me down.
PKD: All right, I'll get you a job on **Blade Runner.** That's what you want. (General hilarity)

* * * * *

(Of course I realize now all history will curse me for not pressing Phil harder for details, but then, how can anyone foresee the future?

(Philip K. Dick, by the way, was born on Beethoven's birthday, 1928).

* * * * *

CHAPTER 34
"We Die Too Soon"

(To conclude then, an extract from a much longer conversation we had about death).

4-22-81

PKD: The fallacy (in complaining about the inevitability of death) really is -- the same point could be made about a movie. If you go to see a movie eventually they'll flash a sign up on the screen saying "The End," and therefore you (say you've) been cheated, in coming to the movie. Because you say I went in, I sat there for an hour and a half, and all of a sudden they flash up the credits.

And I say, did you expect the movie to go on forever, and they say yes, and I say why? And they say, well, I don't know why. I say it's a gratuitous assumption that the movie should go on forever. The movie has a time span in which it unfolds its total process. At that point the movie ends. The movie doesn't end in the middle of the process. It ends after the process has fulfilled itself, not exhausted itself.

But then I respond that it is not a good analogy because life is cut off in the middle, life is truncated. The most informed theological thought, or philosophical thought for that matter, is that death is not the tragedy. Untimely death is the tragedy.

This is what the ancients were trying to overcome, in the mystery religions, was not death, but untimely death. This is what the Tao has to offer us: the tragedy is not that we die, the tragedy is that we die too soon, that is before we can accomplish our purpose.

But then I respond to that, and say how can we define our purpose, we don't even know what our purpose is. How can we be sure when our purpose has been fulfilled? Is it a subjective feeling, or is there some objective criterion by which this can be established?

* * * * *

There is no such thing as timely death, not really.

-- Philip K. Dick
December 16, 1928 -
March 2, 1982

APPENDICES

APPENDIX A
THE NOVELS OF PHILIP K. DICK
all paperback originals unless indicated with (*). The name in parenthesis is that of the original publishing company.

- 1955 **Solar Lottery** (Ace)
- 1956 **The World Jones Made** (Ace)
  The Man Who Japed (Ace)
- 1957 **Eye in the Sky** (Ace)
  The Cosmic Puppets (Ace)
- 1959 **Time Out of Joint** (Lippincott)*
- 1960 **Dr. Futurity** (Ace)
  Vulcan's Hammer (Ace)
- 1962 **The Man in the High Castle** (Putnam)*
- 1963 **The Game Players of Titan** (Ace)
- 1965 **Martian Time-Slip** (Ballantine)
  The Penultimate Truth (Belmont)
  The Simulacra (Ace)
  Clans of the Alphane Moon (Ace)
- 1965 **The Three Stigmata of Palmer Eldritch** (Doubleday)
  Dr. Bloodmoney (Ace)
- 1966 **The Crack in Space** (Ace)
  The Unteleported Man (Ace)
  Now Wait for Last Year (Doubleday)
- 1967 **The Zap Gun** (Pyramid)
  Counter-Clock World (Berkley)
  The Ganymede Takeover (with Ray Nelson) (Ace)
- 1968 **Do Androids Dream of Electric Sheep?** (Doubleday)*
- 1969 **Ubik** (Doubleday)*
  Galactic Pot Healer (Berkley)
- 1970 **Our Friends from Frolix 8** (Ace)
  A Maze of Death (Doubleday)*
- 1972 **We Can Build You** (DAW)
- 1974 **Flow My Tears, the Policeman Said** (Doubleday)*
- 1975 **Confessions of a Crap Artist** (Entwhistle Books)*
- 1976 **Deus Irae** (with Roger Zelazny) (Doubleday)*
- 1977 **A Scanner Darkly** (Ballantine)*
- 1981 **VALIS** (Bantam)
  The Divine Invasion (Simon and Schuster)*
- 1982 **The Transmigration of Timothy Archer** (Simon and Schuster)*
- 1984 **The Man Whose Teeth Were All Exactly Alike** (Mark Ziesing)*
  Lies, Inc. (revision of The Unteleported Man) (Gollancz)*

ANNOUNCED:
In Milton Lumky Territory (Dragon Press)*
Puttering About in a Small Land (Academy Chicago)*

SHORT STORY COLLECTIONS

1955 **A Handful of Darkness** (London: Rich and Cowan)
1957 **The Variable Man and Other Stories** (Ace)
1969 **The Preserving Machine and Other Stories** (Ace)
1973 **The Book of Philip K. Dick** (DAW) (same collection, same year, **The Turning Wheel and Other Stories**, London: Hodder & Stoughton)
1977 **The Best of Philip K. Dick** (Ballantine)
1980 **The Golden Man** (Berkley)
1984 **I Hope I Shall Arrive Soon** (Doubleday)*
Robots, Androids, and Mechanical Oddities (Southern Illinois University Press)*

ANNOUNCED:
The Collected Short Stories of Philip K. Dick (Jeff Conner).*

* * * * *

For complete bibliographical information on Philip Dick's novels and stories, see Daniel J. H. Levack's **PKD: A Phillip K. Dick Bibliography,** with annotations by Steven Owen Godersky (Underwood/Miller, 1981).

APPENDIX B
BIBLIOGRAPHY
The following sources were of help to me in preparing this book. I provide annotations for the curious reader.

INTERVIEWS WITH PHILIP K. DICK

John Boonstra, "Philip K. Dick 1928-1982," **Twilight Zone** 2 (June 1982), pp. 47-52. On **Blade Runner, VALIS,** and his literary career. Good.

Vic Bulluck, "PKD," **Blade Runner Souvenir Magazine** Volume 1. (New York: Ira Friedman, Inc., 1982), p. 8. One page of (positive) reaction to the early footage.

Arthur Byron Cover, "Vertex Interviews Philip K. Dick," **Vertex** (February 1974), p. 34 ff. Good interview, mostly on drugs and the **I-Ching.**

Daniel DePrez, "An Interview with Philip K. Dick," **Science Fiction Review** 19 (August 1976), pp. 6-12. Oddly enough, this interview was supposed to have been made on September 10, 1976 -- now wait for next year? Very good interview, on his writing habits, **A Scanner Darkly,** and his philosophy.

Charles Platt, "Philip K. Dick," **Dream Makers** (New York: Berkley Books, 1980). Essential.

_____, "Reality in Drag," **Science Fiction Review** 36 (August 1980). The same interview as above.

Gregg Rickman, "A Visit with Philip K. Dick," **Uncle Jam** (Long Beach, CA) Vol. 8, No. 50 (July 1981), p. 5 ff. Incorporated into this volume.

_____, "Philip K. Dick's Last Interview," **Uncle Jam** Vol. 9, No. 57 (May 1982), pp. 21-2. Mostly on the Maitreya. To be incorporated into **Philip K. Dick: The Last Testament.**

Slash Vol. 3, No. 5 (1980), pp. 37-8. Good interview from an anonymous scribe in the defunct punk 'zine. On life in his apartment building, politics, and his empathy with dying animals. Thanks to Joe Kaufman for finding this.

James Van Hise, **Starlog** #55. I have the transcript of the complete interview, of August 29, 1981, kindly sent me by Mr. Van Hise. Entirely on **Blade Runner.**

Paul Willaims, "The True Stories of Philip K. Dick," **Rolling Stone** (November 6, 1975), p. 45 ff. Essential: on the 1971 break-in, drugs, his career, with a nice portrait of the author at home with Tessa and Christopher.

BOOKS ON PHILIP K. DICK

Bruce Gillespie, ed. **Philip K. Dick: Electric Shepherd** (Carlton, Victoria, Australia: Nostrilia Press, 1975), 106 pp. "Best of SF Commentary Number 1" -- reprints from the Australian magazine. Must have, for the Introduction by Roger Zelazny, a curious and famous piece by Stanislaw Lem, and above all for the letters to Gillespie from Phil Dick. Also, and vitally, the 1972 Vancouver speech, "The Android and the Human."

Damon Knight, **In Search of Wonder** (Chicago: Advent, 1967. 2nd edition). pp. 228-35. Phil's early novels are discussed in a chapter entitled "Decadents," which gives some idea how the s.f. establishment viewed such dangerous men as Dick, van Vogt, and Alfred Bester. Actually Knight is a sharp and perceptive writer.

Daniel J. H. Levack, **PKD A Philip K. Dick Bibliography.** See reference in Appendix A. A must have for anyone serious about this author.

Joseph D. Olander and Martin Harry Greenberg, **Philip K. Dick** (New York: Taplinger Publishing, 1983), 256 pp. Pretty good sample of received opinion on Dick as of his death. Academic pieces that average highly. Dick discusses his annoyance with a Darko Suvin piece that appears here in Chapter 11 of this book, and took time to ridicule Peter Fitting's Marxist analysis in the DePrez interview cited above. "Writers of the 21st Century" series.

Hazel Pierce, **Philip K. Dick** (Mercer Island, Washington: Starmont House, 1982), 55 pp. Good concise overview, very useful chronology and bibliography. "Starmont Readers Guide 12."

Angus Taylor, **Philip K. Dick and the Umbrella of Light** (Baltimore: T-K Graphics, 1975), 48 pp. Good monograph, emphasizing Dick's mysticism. "SF Author Studies 1."

Patricia S. Warrick, **The Cybernetic Imagination in Science Fiction** (Cambridge: The MIT Press, 1980), pp. 206-30. This solid, humanist-oriented section on "Philip K. Dick's Robots" is essentially identical with a Warrick piece appearing in the Olander-Greenberg anthology.

MISCELLANEOUS REFERENCES

Space prohibits listing all of the many articles, essays, book reviews and so on containing pieces of interest. Here are the most valuable:

Locus, Issue #256, Vol. 15, No. 5 (May 1982) "Philip K. Dick Appreciations." Many of the biggest names in s.f. pay tribute to their fallen comrade. See also **Foundation** 27 (Feburary 1983) and **Science Fiction Chronicle** Vol. 3, No. 8 (May 1982) for more of the same.

Science-Fiction Studies 5 (March 1975) and 32 (March 1984) - operating from a quasi-Marxist perspective - and **Foundation** 26 (October 1982) provide issues featuring much Dickian academic analysis. See also individual articles scattered hither and yon in these magazines and also **Extrapolation** (a good piece by Robert Galbreath in the Summer 1983 issue). And so on.

Two more individual articles demand mention, Paul Sammon's "The Making of **Blade Runner**" in **Cinefantastique** (July-August 1982), with many quotes from Dick, and Gregory Sandow's curious memoir-obit in the **Village Voice** "Voice Literary Supplement" (August 1982). **Timothy Archer** is "a meditation on death so thorough that the only thing left for the man who wrote it was to die." Oh.

Rick Winston sent me the first chapter of a thesis he wrote, or is writing, on Philip K. Dick's use of the **idios** and **koinos cosmos** that looks interesting.

And finally, no Philip K. Dick fan can be without the invaluable information contained in Paul Williams' **The Philip K. Dick Society Newsletter,** available from the PKDS at Box 611, Glen Ellen, CA 95442, for $5 a year. News, memoirs, some fugitive and surprising pieces by PKD himself. Absolutely and completely, totally and utterly essential.

* * * * *

APPENDIX C
TWO LETTERS FROM PHILIP K. DICK

June 26, 1981

Dear Gregg,

Thanks so much for sending me a copy of the published interview. It is great (God, I write a wooden letter). (The reason is, I have the fucking flu and am weak, very weak; I've been in bed for days.) The reason I have the flu is that I sent off my new novel, BISHOP TIMOTHY ARCHER, after working like a maniac on it; I wrote the final 90 pages in 2 days. Hartwell had said, "Everything depends on your getting a completed MS to me RIGHT AWAY," so I just plain killed myself completing it. I lived on French coffee, Scotch, aspirin, and pastrami sandwiches. Well, I got the MS finished, sent it off, and found that my agent was on vacation. He took the MS with him, phoned me and said that he found it unreadable, the first novel he had ever tried but failed to read. Even Gertrude Stein hadn't baffled him, nor James Joyce. I was crushed. He said not to expect to hear from him for a long time because for 5 days he'd tried to read the MS and simply couldn't; he'd given up and gone for long walks. When he got back to his office finally he phoned simply to say he'd read it, and gave virtually no comment. He sent it on to Hartwell, but Hartwell is on vacation -- three weeks. Hartwell took the MS with him. No report; only silence. Meanwhile I began showing signs of the mental and physical strain combined; I began to bleed gastro-intestinally. No more Scotch. No more aspirin. No more pastrami sandwiches. The coffee I can't give up. I was really scared; I had pushed myself too far, and what did I have to show for it? A novel MS my own agent couldn't read. "There is just no audience for this," he told me. "Very few people are going to be willing to try to read this." And, as you know, I'm getting only $7,500. The very real possibility was now presenting itself that when finally given a contract for a "quality" novel I couldn't hack it, and as you also know, I turned down the $400,000 cheapo novelization for BLADE RUNNER, so I may have made a compound mistake, not a simple mistake. I am still waiting for Hartwell to respond; meanwhile I keep looking over the BISHOP TIMOTHY ARCHER MS to see what's so hard to read about it. It's definitely an interior viewpoint, as we discuss in the interview. It is indeed hard going. But the characterization is superb! The character of the protagonist Angel Archer really comes off, as does the Bishop himself; the interaction between the two of them is terrific, the best writing I've ever done. The scene in which she learns that the Bishop has died in the Dead Sea Desrt in Israel is one of the best scenes in modern literature. Yet I ask myself, "What is this all for?" My health is wrecked, literally; I am in bed most of the time, now, wasted and fucked up, living on yogurt. I will never be able to drink that 12 year old Scotch again that I love so much. I put everything I had into the novel and I feel as if I've pissed on the carpet and everyone in New York is ashamed for my sake, embarrassed by what I've done. And I'm missing out on the big bucks. HOWEVER, your letter and the interview **enormously** cheered me up; it is such a great interview, and there is such good news in your letter -- congratulations on placing the article that started off our friendship! Wonderful! That really makes me feel the universe is not a bad place after all, that there **is** some dim form of theodicy. I perceived you as one of the great new talents in the field of criticism, and it makes me think back to how Tony Boucher must have felt in 1951 when I sent F&SF that first story, BEYOND LIES THE -- no, wrong, ROOG. That's it; ROOG. And he bought it. I see in you a great career lying ahead, a person not only with talent but with integrity (spelling?). I want to see you define me and my role in writing, my limitations and my contributions, what I did that was original, where I failed, where I succeeded, what I cared about, what mattered to me. One day I'll be gone and you'll be there writing away and how I'm remembered and thought of will (I'm am convinced) depend to a great degree on how you specifically see me...and you will be doing - and probably already are doing - this with other people in writing and in film-making. Recently, to make my point, I got another academic article dealing with my stuff, and man, it is dreadful. It is just whale shit, or squid ink, amorphous and dull and -- well, you know how I feel. I'm really glad you liked THE DIVINE INVASION; yes, it is a happy book, and it does answer all the objections that Ursula raised. Meanwhile VALIS is selling extraordinarily well. The original 85,000 copy edition sold right out, plumb sold out in a couple of weeks; it was #2 on the **Locus** bestseller list. Bantam ran off a 27,000 copy second edition; it sold out. They ran off a third edition, 25,000 more copies. Bantam is very pleased. **We,** Russ and I, are very pleased. I guess I should be pleased that I did get the BISHOP TIMOTHY ARCHER novel written, because (as we discuss in your interview) I had stopped dead in my tracks on page 3. But I feel mortality closing in on me; I was physically hurting, literally, when I finished it, and I knew that the days in which I could speed-rush a novel into existence were gone, gone, gone. Age is the name of the tune they are playing, age and fatigue. "Time's winged chariot." Wow, do I sense it. But damn it, I got the novel finished! What if I'd dropped before finishing it? I was talking to one of my ex-wives on the phone last week, and she told me that an old drinking buddy of mine had died, died from liver damage due to drink. It terrified me. There is nothing romantic about bleeding to death, as he did. I set down the phone, called up Tessa and asked her if she thought I'd bit the big one. No, she said; just rest awhile. Take it easy...I paid $65,00 in income taxes for 1980; I had bought myself no luxuries during the year except for the Scotch. Shit! Well, I blame BLADE RUNNER; negotiating with them has worn me down. They withdrew their permission for us to use their logo rights with DO ANDROIDS DREAM. We said we'd publish it anyhow. They responded with the following deal: we would get the logo rights but instead of the royalty split being 8% to me and 2% to them, it would be 6% to them and 4% to me, so instead of my advance being $25,000 I'd get only half that and so on down the line. Well, they asked, would he like to reconsider doing the novelization, this being the case? I said to Russ, "Tell them to go fuck themselves" and then I started bleeding. Negotiations continue. We may wind up with a 5%-5% split, and we'll have the logo rights and sell a million copies of the original novel. But Tinsel Town will kill you, they will run over you like a fucking truck. Russ says that their negotiator is a foxy 27 year-old chick named Debbie...Debbie showed my agent many lovley (sp?) lovely pictures of the sets, which my agent reports are simply stunning. So is Debbie. I was supposed to phone her up when she got back to the West Coast "And she will be your Virgil to Dante showing you around **Inferno**," my agent said happily, as if a trip through **Inferno** were a-ok just so long as some fox is your psychopomp. I'm afraid to meet Debbie. She'll run circles around me. I know when I'm outgunned. I keep saying, "But I did finish the Bishop Archer novel novel. I did, I did." And David Hartwell may not like it. That is wipe-out city. Had my chance and blew it. But ah, your interview and letter! What a joy! I reread both again and again. I love the typo "gookstore." The best newspaper typo I ever heard of is as follows (it appeared in a Fullerton newspaper around 1973): "Chicken farts 49¢ a pound." Which means that, like souls, chicken farts must weigh something.

I'm going to be okay, Gregg (lest all this Sturm und Drang is worrying you). I am just sort of angry. In my mind is a master plan in which I turn down the BLADE RUNNER offer, do the Bishop Archer novel instead, and, as a result, am remembered forever as a great artist, but now I'm beginning to see a somewhat different outcome: I am not remembered as a great artist because the Bishop Archer novel is a failure and on top of that the effort expended in getting it written right away kills me, so I am neither great nor alive. "Better a live dog than a dead lion," but I would be a dead **dog**. (As in THE DIVINE INVASION.) Yet that dog's death had importance, as I discuss in that novel. I am so pleased to see your career going good, because, see, the torch has to be passed on to the new, the young, the talented, the energetic (and from the old, the talented, the burned-out), and that is what I am , due to writing BTA, burned out. But oh those last 90 pages! When Angel hears of the Bishop's death and turns into a machine as a result, ceases (herself) to be human any longer, due to his death. She will be a machine that repeats what it has heard, as she puts it. Nothing new will ever arise in its heart and mind, now; it is a machine -- but this changes when the Sufi guru Edgar Barefoot (whose seminar she is attending) singles her out and speaks to her, calls forth that great soul of hers into life once more, summons it back into being, out of its mortification.

Okay, Gregg, you're off and running; congratulations, and I feel I'm proved right in my estimation of your talent. There's no turning back for you now, my man; you're too good, you have too much to say. Excuse the self-indulgence in this letter; blame the flu and blame the fact that I'm waiting on pins and needles to hear from Dave Hartwell. I will hear, and if he doesn't like the novel, well, there are other editors (also there are other novels). I got a lot out of writing it and reading it over; Angel Archer is real to me, totally real; I love her and respect her; she is intelligent, scrappy, funny, original, tender, kind, and there never was anyone like her in literature before. I don't know where I got her from; maybe Angel Archer is my own soul.

Affectionately, Phil

* * * * *

June 29, 1981

Dear Gregg,

A short letter to let you know that I heard from David Hartwell that my BISHOP TIMOTHY ARCHER novel is "excellent" and that he is "delighted," so we have a wrap. Later tonight Paul Williams, our mutual friend, phoned me to tell me more details. David liked the first 100 pages the most, and was initially dubious about the ending, but finally came to see it as okay. (Actually, in my opinion the ending is the best part, but what the hell; he did finally decide to take it as it is.) So everything has turned out okay.

I saw a short clip of BLADE RUNNER tonight on the Channel Four news, a segment on Douglas Trumbull (who as you know did the special effects). The damn thing terrified me; Trumbull has totally caught the Phil Dick desolated urban environment of tomorrow; it was as if my brain was projecting its worldview onto my TV screen! At once I knew what I was seeing, and sure enough, they then identified it as BLADE RUNNER. But how would you feel if you were sitting there eating dinner and idly watching the TV, and all of a sudden you saw your own private nightmare world on the screen? It is obvious to me that my Worldview of modern California urban sprawl is based on my having read THE TIBETIAN BOOK OF THE DEAD: the smoky red light, the dark swirls of grit. Trumbull described it as "dirty and grungy. This is not a clean environment." Well, it is Dante's **Inferno,** is what it is, and in 1974 when I had my supernatural experiences on which VALIS is based I saw our world literally as hell, as what I have been calling the Black Iron Prison. This is eerie. My novel-in-progress assumes that the three realms of Dante's COMMEDIA are three ways of viewing reality, **this** life, not the next; I got this idea from reading comments by Dante on the COMMEDIA; he **said** that the three realms are in this world. This is a Sufi notion, a very mystical, very secret comprehension that now we are dead and in a kind of prison (Plato quotes a "very old wise man, probably an Orphic," as telling him this). **Inferno** is characterized by metal, by dark clouds, the smoky red light, immutable cause-and-effect, total repetition, total karmic control, total recycling of everything forever, as if time has stopped. In **Purgatorio** - get this! - **time runs backward.** And there is some freedom. This is a realm that partakes half of **Inferno** and half of **Paradiso**; it is a mixture. The mode is walking. Some change exists. Karma has power but can be broken by the right acts (in **Inferno** nothing you do will break your programming; you are a machine world). When you perform the right act, instantly the karmic fetters loosen. The colors lighten. Brightness enters. The mode is flying, not walking. Time flows forward; there is constant newness. BLADE RUNNER captures **Inferno** with no hint of redemption. In **Inferno** your only hope is an adventitious savior entering; there is nothing you yourself can do to free yourself. My supernatural experiences in March, 1974 on which VALIS is based can be understood as my being sprung from **Purgatorio** by the merit of an act that I performed; I was thereby transferred out of **Purgatorio,** or at least into one of the higher levels, perhaps even the highest level, that of Earthly Delight, the Palm Tree Garden; I heard what Dante reports: the lady singing, and I drank from the fountain of anamnesis (recollection). All this fits in with Sufi mysticism, but not with Christian or for that matter any other that I know of, but Dante was strongly influenced by the Sufis. This is why, as you noted, THE DIVINE INVASION has an optimism that virtually is absent in all my previous writing; in that novel I am experiencing the Garden to which I was taken upon remembering **Inferno,** the Black Iron prison; I had not merely been sprung from **Purgatorio**; I had been sprung from **Inferno,** and this (as I say) cannot be done by one's own efforts but requires the Savior's intervention; it is a reprieve of an otherwise eternal sentence; so being sprung from **Inferno** is an extraordinary event and perhaps related to the Parousia at the End Days). Seeing the short clip from BLADE RUNNER I realized that in all my writing I have been saying that we are dead and in hell; this is especially true of UBIK where my message becomes explicit. And, in UBIK, the savior enters in the form of Runciter's messages (that would be Christ) and Ubik itself (that would be God). The Orphic-Pythagorean utterances that Plato quotes ("Now we are dead and in a kind of prison" which is expressed also as by "the body is the tomb of the soul") means specifically that we are in hell; we are not just dead; we are being punished, and the Gnostics called this heimarmene, which is a word difficult to translate but refers to a combination of the power of the Mosaic Torah (Law) and the causality, that is astral determinism of fate (ananke). All this will show up in my new novel, THE OWL IN DAYLIGHT. Very strange, Gregg. Dante is our guide; the solution to the mystery of our corporeal existence, our servitude, lies in the COMMEDIA, yet everyone assumes it has to do with the **next** world; we read it and do not recognize our condition. The three realms are what I term coaxial realities; that is, there is no spatiotemporal difference between them, only ontological difference. People living in **Inferno** live in a sense in the same world as those living in **Purgatorio** and **Paradiso** but each person experiences this matrix reality differently; some experience it as hell, and there are many levels of this; some as purgatory, with its many levels, etc. This is dealt with by the European existential psychiatrists after the fashion of Heidegger: in terms of ontology, levels of ontology, the three realms being surnamed **Umwelt (Inferno)**, **Miltwelt (Purgatorio)**, and finally **Eigenwelt (Paradiso)**. This relates directly to the conviction I have eternally held that people experience world (Dasein) radically differently. So in March, 1974 I remember **Inferno** (the Black Iron Prison), but was quickly moved to the Palm Tree Garden. Do you think this wil make an interesting novel? I hope so; Hartwell is paying me three times for it what he's paying for BISHOP TIMOTHY ARCHER. It had damn well better be good!

Phil Dick

P.S.: It really freaked me to see that clip of BLADE RUNNER, as you can see by this letter. My God; the world I write about is hell. Literally. And anyone with any sense will recognize it when they see the movie; Trumbull has caught it absolutely. How extraordinary -- what genius!!

(The "published interview" Phil refers to in the first letter is the first **Uncle Jam** interview, July 1981 -- with the typo "gookstore" for "bookstore." The "placed article" is the **Caritas** essay, which was accepted by an academic publisher for an anthology -- which never came out.

(With all this embarassing praise Phil heaps on me I should point out, that in reading through his correspondence, I found that he tended to speak in hyperbole - "you're my best friend," etc. - to many people, some virtually strangers. Nevertheless I have been profoundly moved and inspired by Phil's praise of me -- I feel I owe him an enormous debt, not just for our friendship, but for his work as an author and his stature as a human being -- and I have tried my best, in this book, to justify his words to me).

* * * * *

ABOUT THE AUTHOR

GREGG RICKMAN was born in Santa Monica, California. He has worked in a health food store, as a library clerk, as a teacher of creative writing and of film making to children, as a recreation aide (checker player) with seniors, and as a writer. He has written quantities of film criticism and a good deal of journalism; he has also made several independent (Super 8 and video) films. He is truly, say his friends, a hard working boy. This is his first book.

More PKD...

2nd book: **PHILIP K. DICK: THE LAST TESTAMENT by Gregg Rickman.**
Foreword by Robert Silverberg.
Publication date: Sept. 1984.
3rd book: **PHILIP K. DICK: A LIFE by Gregg Rickman.** Details and publication to date to be announced (Spring 1985)

To order your copy of send **$9.95** (CA residents include 6½% sales tax), check or money order to **Fragments West,** 3908 East 4th Street, Long Beach, Calif. 90814.

Frank the Unicorn

Book One: The Adventures Of a Modern Day Unicorn by Phil Yeh
Gail's a struggling actress, Bernie's a struggling writer, Tisa's a struggling feminist, Frank is a Unicorn; he doesn't struggle except when he's on the golf course. The book takes place in New York City, San Francisco, and Los Angeles.
Book #1 - 80 pages, 5¼" x 8½" Quality softcover - $4.95

Book Two: **Frank On The Farm** by Phil Yeh
This book includes a fantastic foreword by **Mad Magazine's Sergio Aragones** (worth the price of the whole book!). Frank and his friends travel throughout the Pacific Northwest and the Golden State of California visiting Seattle, Port Townsend, Portland, Shasta, Nevada City, even Victoria, Canada as well as all those crazy places in Southern California. If you don't laugh twelve times a second, you're not normal.
Book #2 - 80 pages 5¼" x 8½" Quality softcover - $4.95

Book Three: **Mr. Frank Goes to Washington, D.C** by Phil Yeh
This book is a February 1984 release - just in time for all the real humor of the presidential elections in America. No, Frank isn't running for office, he's simply trying to find a good golf course. In this book, everything that you've always wondered about in the American Government will be explained, once and for all.
Book #3 80 pages 5¼" x 8½" Quality softcover - $4.95.

Look for two other Frank books out in 1984!

- - - - - - - - - - - - - - - - - - -

HEY! I want to find out what the whole world is gonna be talking about before everyone starts talking about it. Send me the following **Frank The Unicorn** books. I understand that if I don't laugh at least 3,490 times during each book, I can **try** and get my money back (wow!).

Send me #1 _____ #2 _____ #3 _____ at **$4.95 for each copy ordered.** California residents add 6½% sales tax. We pay the postage and Phil will sign every book ordered through this ad.
Send check or money order to: **FRAGMENTS WEST, 3908 East Fourth Street, Long Beach, California 90814.**

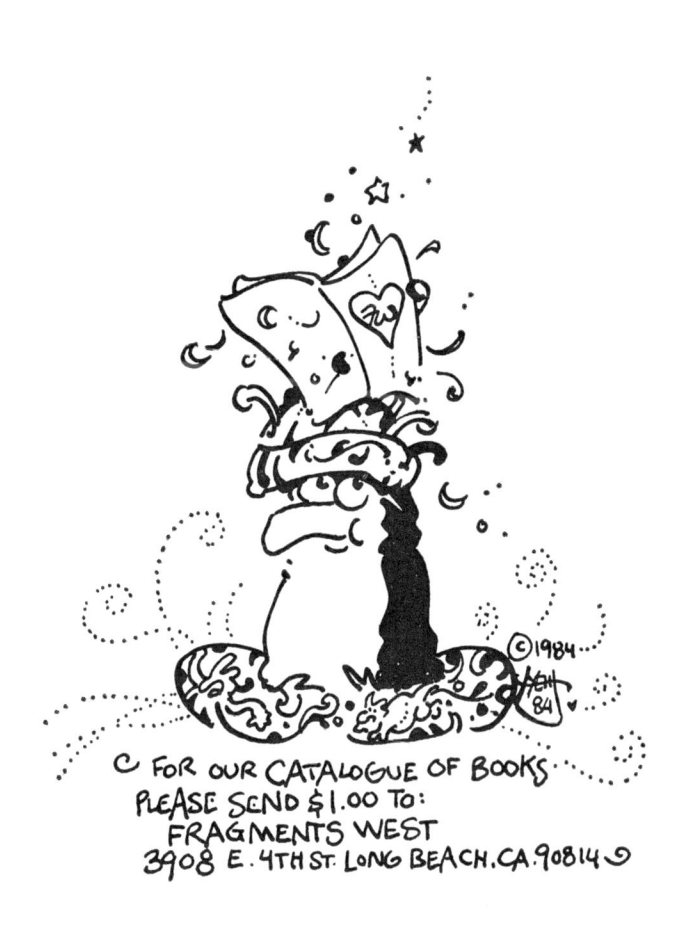

FRAGMENTS WEST